DON'T LOOK BACK

Robert V. Ward, Jr.

"DON'T LOOK BACK"
Copyright August 2007

By
Robert V. Ward, Jr.

Dedicated to the memory of Elsie and Eleanor.

Prologue

My name is Roger Work. For nearly two decades, I was a successful Criminal Defense Attorney. A phone call changed all of that. That call turned my world upside down. Friends use to say to me "You can take the man out of Philly but you can't take the Philly out of the man." Apparently, they were right.

My saintly Grandmother, Sadie, once told me, "Condemn the sin but not the sinner. I didn't get it then. But now, I do.

The story that you are about to read chronicles my fall from grace and my attempt to find redemption. Sadie tried to show me the way. I was always a good student in terms of book learning. However, many of the lessons that Sadie tried to impart fell on deaf ears. In the end of course, Grandma Sadie was right about sinners and a great deal more. I now have a new found respect for the teachings one gets from the "School of Hard Knocks."

Chapter 1
"Love Is A Hurtin' Thing"

The steel cell door clanked shut and the correction's officer shouted into his shoulder microphone, "Dead man in."

Roger Work, Jr. had returned to his cell after his shower and the morning count. Daily showers, thirty minutes in the recreation yard per week, and periodic trips to the law library were the only times that Roger Jr. was allowed out of his cell. For Roger, M.C. Waynesburg Penitentiary was a living hell and he was doomed to remain there until his execution. Before his first-degree murder conviction, Roger had been a criminal attorney, well respected in his field. What a difference a day can make!

Even though he was a lawyer, Roger was ill-prepared for prison and life on death row. A somewhat gregarious person, he feared that the extreme isolation, in part, the by-product of one inmate per cell plus the normal routine at Waynesburg would drive him insane.

Convicted of first-degree murder in a Philadelphia court, Roger had practiced law exclusively in Baltimore. A death sentence for killing another black man was about as rare as the sighting of Hailey's Comet. Roger had never considered himself lucky, but somehow he'd managed to do what few others in his position had accomplished, namely, to get a death sentence for killing another black man. The phrase, "It's better to be lucky than good-looking," rattled around in his head. He had picked the wrong time to get lucky. It frightened Roger to think that the next time he might be outside of Waynesburg is when the state would ship his lifeless body home for burial. Roger had been transferred from Philly to Waynesburg, a maximum security prison located in western Pennsylvania for convicted murderers sentenced to death while awaiting the results of his mandatory appeal.

When Roger first arrived at Waynesburg, he had some regular visitors. His wife, Irene and niece, Brandi were the most frequent. Homeboys J.T. and Eric also occasionally visited. Now, after spending nearly three years at Waynesburg, the frequency of visits by family and friends had reduced to a mere trickle. The ten-hour drive -- 526 miles round trip between Philly and the prison -- discouraged regular visits.

Roger promised his grandmother, Sadie, "I will make the most of my time while waiting the final word on my execution."

While incarcerated, Roger devoted his time to getting in shape. Where there once had been a flabby, bald-headed black man, Roger, at age fifty, was now trim and lean. Two-hundred push-ups and sit-ups a day will do that for you. He also learned to do yoga to keep his mind clear. Roger, who had never been a health nut or gym freak was in the best shape of his life. The irony was not lost on him. "Shit, now that I'm really healthy, the state's preparing a lethal injection for me." Roger mumbled to himself, "Who said that the Gods lack a sense of humor?" As for his mental health, Roger found that helping his fellow inmates with their legal problems during his trips to the law library allowed him to feel better. None of this, however, was an adequate substitute for being away from the people he loved. At times his heart ached to see them.

When Roger returned to his cell after his shower, he spotted two envelopes on his bunk. Even junk mail was viewed as a pleasant break from the daily drudgery of prison life. He turned his attention to the two pieces. Both were legal documents. They were "virgin," meaning that correctional officials hadn't opened either to review its content. Roger was excited to hear from the world outside the walls of Waynesburg.

The first letter was from the Circuit Court in Baltimore, Maryland, the other from Pennsylvania's Supreme Court. Roger opened the Baltimore mail first. In the legal caption he read "Final Notice to Irene Work, plaintiff versus Roger Work, Jr., defendant. The marriage between the parties is dissolved effective November 9, 2005."

Both Roger and Irene used to tell each other, "Our storybook romance will last forever." Roger and Irene met their first year of law school in Delaware. At the time, both were starry eyed and full of idealism. Irene, a white spitfire, was petite with curly dark hair. She was reared in Redrock, Utah and wanted to be a community organizer and work with undocumented immigrants. There was no doubt in Roger's mind that Irene would succeed. Roger, back then, was tall and fat with a "Dr. J" - style afro. He planned to make his money representing white-collar criminals. Sometimes opposites attract. Irene and Roger fit the mold of country girl and city slicker. Roger had grown up in North Philly in the area formally known as Strawberry Mansion but now, sarcastically, called Blackberry Mansion. The name stuck after the neighborhood had turned over in the wake of White Flight. It was a tough area. Largely, because of the love and guidance of his grandmother, Sadie, and Big Roger, his Dad, Roger managed to graduate from high school, college and law school. He had been lucky to have escaped "The Hood." Sometimes, late at night, Roger would share with Irene just how difficult and sad life had been in Philly. He told her, "Most of my posse, my homeboys, didn't live past thirty."

Roger and Irene began dating in their second year of school. Upon graduation, they shacked-up in a Baltimore townhouse. Irene went to work immediately for Legal Services in Washington, DC. Roger struggled to find work. He could recall like it was yesterday, rushing home one evening to tell Irene, "I landed a position with Coleman, Healy and Tisler, a thirty-attorney firm in downtown Baltimore. Coleman, Healy and Tisler specialize in the defending of white-collar criminals, slippery clients with big bucks."

Irene and Roger married a few years after each had established their respective practices. Their ceremony took place before a small assembly of friends and relatives. The couple's first dance was to Lou Rawls' crooning "Love Is A Hurtin' Thing." Theirs was a solid marriage. As "DINKS," double income no kids, they could afford two houses, one on the Maryland shore and the other in an upscale neighborhood in west Baltimore. The waterfront house was their hideaway.

Irene stood by Roger's side throughout the murder trial. They cried together after the verdict was announced. A few months into Roger's incarceration, the couple began to discuss the topic of divorce. "Irene, you know how much I love you, but this "death-row" thing means no conjugal visits. You stood by me throughout this mess. You're a fine lookin' woman, beautiful, youthful and vibrant. You should forget about me and move on with your life. Nobody can ever take away what we had." Irene protested but ultimately, she recognized that he was right. Eventually, they agreed on a no-fault divorce.

Irene kept the house near Baltimore and they agreed to sell the place on the shore. Both had comfortable 401K's so there was no haggling over assets. With the sale of the house, Irene walked away from the marriage half a million to the better. She'd also get Roger's 401K upon his death. Roger was satisfied with his two hundred and fifty thousand. Also, he owned his grandmother's house which Sadie had left to him upon her death. Roger felt like a millionaire. This was bitter sweet. Soon, he'd be a wealthy dead man. At what was expected to be one of their last conversations, Roger, known for his dry wit, told Irene: "Don't worry, honey, things could be worse...I could be black, dead and poor."

As Roger looked at the document, he could feel his emotions bubbling to the surface. Since there's no crying in prison, he opened the other letter. It too was a Notice. His appeal before the Pennsylvania Supreme Court was scheduled to be heard in less than ninety days. Roger moved over to the bars and shouted for a Correction's Officer. "Hey, I'd like to go to the law library!" A voice shouted back,, "Someone will come to get you shortly." Roger then dropped to the floor to do his second rep of sit-ups. "One, two, three..."

Chapter 2

"Philadelphia Freedom"

During Roger's murder trial, Frank Washington had second-chaired Joyce Franklin as Defense Counsel. Frank's specialty was appellate work. Both were old friends and former classmates of Roger and Irene. They called themselves the "Fearless Four." The Fearless Four actually began as a five-person study group at Southern Delaware School of Law. In their first year of law school, Joyce, Irene, Thom, Frank and Roger were inseparable. They attended classes together, studied together, and played together. Then Thom Dean transferred to a law school in Philly after his first year for family reasons. Nevertheless, the five remained in touch with each other. Thom would eventually help Joyce and Frank secure employment in Philadelphia. However, with Thom's departure, the Fearless Four was solidified as a team. Joyce, Irene, Frank and Roger promised undying loyalty to each other.

Joyce, a black woman about 5'9" in her stocking feet, was attractive and funny. She often reminded people of her hero from Texas, Congresswoman Barbara Jordan. Joyce won the best oral Advocate Award in the National Mock Trial Competition at the end of their second year of school.

Frank asked Joyce to be his partner in the Third-Year Appellate Advocacy Competition. Appellate advocacy was Frank's forte. Frank was a natural. The son of a North Carolina white Baptist minister, Frank helped the four stay grounded. They frequently referred to Frank as "the tortoise" -- slow but sure.

When Irene and Roger married, Joyce and Frank served as Maid of Honor and Best Man. When Roger needed help, there was never any question that Joyce and Frank would represent him at his trial and appeal.

Given the evidence available at trial, a conviction seemed guaranteed. But Roger had the right to an appeal. Frank decided to participate in every phrase of the trial. Because of Frank's attention to detail, he was regarded as one of the best appellate attorneys in the area.

On the same morning that Roger was reading his mail, Frank noticed a small story in the *Daily News* indicating that the owner and bartender at the B & E Tavern, Blake Edwards, had been killed in an attempted robbery.

The following day, Frank stopped by the Philadelphia police headquarters known as "The Roundhouse," to speak with a few officers who were his pals. Casually, they mentioned that according to Ballistics, the gun found near Blake had been tied to a number of shootings where Larry had possible involvement. Larry was the man that Roger had shot to death to earn his spot on death row. The officers were certain that the gun belonged to Larry, but the Latent Prints Department had yet to issue its report.

Frank asked, "Who caught Blake's case?" He was directed to Detective Jack Pillsbury. Pillsbury didn't know Frank and therefore, was reluctant to share any information with a defense lawyer. Frank suggested that Pillsbury call District Attorney Lynne's office to get the okay."

After a few minutes on the phone verifying that Frank was okay, Pillsbury hung up and told Frank about the gun and the crime scene. Prior to expiring, Blake told the police, "The gun belonged to Larry. On the night that Roger killed Larry, I removed the gun from Larry's coat before the cops arrived." Blake believed that Larry, being armed, would only complicate things for him. "I didn't want to lose my liquor license." Frank thanked Pillsbury for his help and wished him luck with finding Blake's killer.

Two days later, Frank and Joyce filed a motion for a new trial for Roger. In their brief they argued, "Roger Work did not have a fair trial. Given that Larry was armed, Roger should have been able to raise the issue of self defense. He had not."

The officers, when questioned at trial said, "No guns or knives were found on the premises." For reasons that were not apparent, the police didn't find the gun the night Larry died. This wasn't a complete surprise since Larry's gun-toting gang split like cockroaches when a light was turned on once the body hit the floor of the B &E Tavern. Nevertheless, because of this omission, Roger now had a bona fide basis for a new trial.

During the motion session, Judge Earl Brewster of the Common Plea's Court, after listening to both sides said, "I will issue a ruling in two weeks." He urged District Attorney Lynne "to work something out." Joyce drove out to Waynesburg to share the news with Roger.

One week before Roger's case was scheduled to be heard by the Pennsylvania Supreme Court, District Attorney Lynne offered Joyce and Frank a deal. He said, "If Roger pleads guilty to manslaughter rather than press for a new trial, the state would recommend a sentence that amounted to credit for time served, nearly three years and probation for ten years." Joyce and Frank looked at Lynne in disbelief. Regaining their composure they said, "We need to speak with our client." They promised to get back to Lynne in a few days. Lynne was fighting a tough re-election battle and didn't need anyone questioning the competency of his office at this time. Tall and handsome, Lynne had "it." He could have been a movie star. He came from money. Lynne had the looks and the pedigree to be elected Governor someday. A term as a U.S. Senator was not out of the question. Lynne was ambitious. He believed that he could really be somebody with a little luck. He'd been uncomfortable with Roger's case all along and this was a good way to put it behind him. Perhaps more importantly, this action avoided making the police and his office look bad in the media. When Joyce spoke with Roger and told him about the offer, his response was: "Take it. Get me out of this hell hole."

Almost three years to the day that Roger was sentenced to death, he was back in Judge Tasker's courtroom. Judge Tasker went through the usual colloquy. This is where the defendant and the judge pretend that no deal has been struck. Tasker said, "Roger Work, you've been indicted for manslaughter in the death of Larry Sims. Are you prepared to plead guilty?" "Yes, Your Honor." "Are you doing so free and voluntarily?" Roger stated "Yes, Your Honor." Judge Tasker then accepted the plea and imposed the sentence recommended by the Assistant District Attorney sent by Lynne to handle the matter. Once completed, court was adjourned. January 15th would always be thought of as liberation day for the remainder of Roger's life.

Roger was taken back to the holding area in the courthouse to be processed for release. Two hours later, Roger was greeted by Brandi and his two lawyers. Brandi, his only blood-niece, was the second college graduate in the family. Since birth, Brandi had been the sunshine of his life. Roger was extremely pleased about spending his first moments of his freedom with Brandi. There were smiles everywhere when Roger was finally released. After three long years, Roger was about to get his first taste of Philadelphia freedom. Brandi said, "Where to, Uncle?" Roger, without a pause said, "33rd Street, please, Grandma Sadie's house." Sadie was Roger's paternal grandmother. She and her husband Vaughn had been blessed with only one child, Roger, Sr. Big Roger, like his own father, worked for the Reading Railroad. The Reading Railroad was largely a freight carrier. Most Northerners conveniently ignore that Jim Crow also lived in Boston, New York and Philadelphia. The men in the Work family were fortunate to be employed in an industry where racial discrimination was not as tenacious. Sadie was proud of her husband and son. Today, most people only know of the Reading Railroad as a stop on the Monopoly board game.

Roger was going home and he could hardly wait to begin his new life.

Chapter 3

"Sadie"

Roger got into the passenger side of Brandi's mini-van. "Are you ready Uncle?"

"I've been ready."

Brandi drove from the courthouse in Center City toward Grandma Sadie's house in North Philly. Surprisingly, the mini van contained several bags of groceries. Brandi said, "They're for you, Uncle." From the Parkway, which was surrounded by museums and fountains, she picked up Interstate 76 West. They exited I-76 at Girard Avenue. To their left was the Philadelphia Zoo, the oldest zoo in the Country. Turning right on Girard Avenue, Brandi then veered left onto 33rd Street. Once there, she and Roger cruised by the summer home of jazz great, John Coltrane. The neighborhood itself had changed very little since Roger left for college in 1970. To Roger, being there felt like he had traveled back in time. To the right were row houses in various stages of decay and disrepair. On the left was the luscious greenery of Fairmont Park. Fairmount Park is the nation's largest landscaped park. The one positive development that Roger observed was the beautiful wall murals that checkered the area. On the sides of the three-story buildings, one could see wonderful murals of William Penn, Dr. J., Grover Washington, Malcolm X as well as various lesser-known folks who had made significant contributions to the life of the city. It was as though the city itself had become a painter's canvas – a living art museum. Roger thought of this as art amongst the ruins. Gentrification had yet to hit this part of North Philly, but the murals and the park helped to mute what otherwise looked more like Falluja in Iraq, circa 2005.

When Joyce visited Roger at Waynesburg to update him on recent developments in his case, he was hopeful. So much so, that he asked Joyce, who was the trustee of his estate, to assemble a crew to clean up and repair Grandma Sadie's place. He asked her to have the gas, electricity, and phone service restored. Roger figured if he was lucky in court, he'd live there. If not, the property could be sold later. While riding along, Brandi and Roger were chatting. "How are the kids?"

"Fine! They're growing like weeds."

"I look forward to seeing them."

They arrived at 2255 N. 33rd Street, and both got eerily quiet. Sadie had done so much for them. There were so many happy memories associated with the house that it was akin to approaching a holy shrine. Most of Roger's memories of this house were positive. The only sad thoughts associated with it stemmed from when Roger's mother, Alexis, died. Sadie had made sure that as a child, Roger knew that he was loved. She also encouraged her grandchildren and great-granddaughter to take advantage of the arts and culture offered in the city. Roger, Jr. had attended plays and operas and frequented Philly's various art museums. Sadie was fond of saying, "Being poor is a state of mind: one can be poor, but you don't have to act like it." She always encouraged Roger, "Do what is right, even if the whole world is doing their own thing. And remember, above all else, to thy own self be true." As a child, Roger was never exactly sure what this all meant. But he knew that Grandma thought that it was important, so that was good enough for him.

While religious, Sadie was no prude. Sadie liked to have a good time. When she and the "girls," (all women sixty or over) got together, it was party time. They enjoyed having fun and bending an elbow. Her home was always filled with food, drink and interesting people. They'd start to party on a Friday night, and it lasted until church time on Sunday. Sadie loved her beer and scotch, in that order. She also loved to talk about politics and world events.

Brandi and Roger stepped out of the car. It was obvious that Joyce's people had done a nice job on the exterior of the three story house. Roger would enjoy having his morning coffee on the partially enclosed porch and gazing into the park. When they entered the house,

14

they looked about and smiled at each other. They knew instinctively that Sadie would love the restorations to the interior. Roger, now free to rebuild his life, said a quiet prayer of thanks to Sadie as he hugged his niece and said "I love you Sugar."

Roger was at last, free and at home.

There was no "Welcome Wagon" in Roger's neighborhood. But Bessie Johnson is the next best thing. When she knocked on the door and saw Roger, she said, "Child, it is good to see you and Brandi. Sadie would be so happy knowin that her grandchildren were living in her house." "Thank you, Miss Bessie. It is nice to see you too. Would you like a little taste?" "Honey, it's kind of early for me but, if there's still some of Sadie's old stash, I'd be glad to have a little one. You know the block hasn't been the same since Sadie passed. This house was quiet for too long."

Ms. Bessie was 80ish but looked younger. Bessie had two children with her husband, Howard. They also had five grandchildren. One granddaughter died of a drug overdose the previous year. Sadie and Bessie were the first black families to move to the 33rd Street section of Strawberry Mansion.

Miss Bessie was one of Sadie's oldest girlfriends. She sat her ample bottom down at the formal dining room table while Roger poured her a drink. "Sadie had a hard time in those last few weeks, but we girls did the best we could to care for her."

Warmly, Roger said "I know. Thank you so much, we appreciate your effort."

Bessie, now a tad bit embarrassed responded, "You're welcome."

Brandi invited Miss Bessie to stay for supper but after downing her drink, she begged off. As she was leaving, Bessie said, "Roger, you be careful. Things are different now. The drug dealers and addicts seem to be around all of the time. Things are rough around here, so you watch out. One good thing though is little Eric. He's buying up abandoned houses left and right and fix-in them up so that families can move back into the area." When their talk ended, Bessie walked down the street to her own house. Shortly after that, as if on cue, Eric came by to welcome Roger back to the neighborhood. He said, "It is good to see some of the old timers returning. If I can help you out in any way, please let me know." He gave Roger his business card and left.

Brandi had brought along with her steaks, a rub, produce for a salad, rice pilaf and some homemade collard greens. While she reheated the greens, made a salad and prepared the rice, Roger got the grill started in the backyard. Under a tarp was "Bertha," an old charcoal grill that had been in the family for thirty years. For as long as he could remember, the family had been barbequing turkeys, chickens and spare ribs on old Bertha to the delight of friends and neighbors.

When the coals were just right, Roger grilled the steaks. He and Brandi gathered around the table to say grace before breaking bread.

During supper, Brandi said, "Thank you, Uncle, for saving my family." "I'm not proud of shooting a man, even a low-life like your Dad, but you're all I have for family, and, it seemed like the right thing to do then. While out at Waynesburg, I had plenty of time to think about what I did. Maybe I could have handled the situation differently, but what's done is done." For dessert, Brandi and Roger shared a package of devil's food chocolate frosted cupcakes made by Tastykake. Tastykakes are a critical component of the food pyramid in Philly.

When the table was cleared and the dishes cleaned, Brandi said, "I should be getting home to my family." Brandi and Roger embraced, and then she headed home.

After Brandi departed, Roger phoned his ex-wife, Irene. Although no longer married, they still remained friends.

Irene stated, "I'm so happy that you've been released."

Roger told her, "I'm still in a daze. Everything happened so quickly. How's work?" "Things are going well, you know, the usual ups and downs." Carefully, they broached the subject of personal relationships. "Irene, do you have someone special in your life?"

"Yeah, sort of. I met someone but it is still early. I don't know if he's a keeper."

Roger was happy for her. In fact, he felt a sense of relief. Without saying, it was very clear that they would always love each other. But Roger and Irene were comfortable with the idea of moving on in their respective lives.

Irene asked, "Is there anything that you need?"

"No darling, everything is good. I'm looking forward to living a normal life. Of course, I'll have to stay in Philly while on probation, but I believe that things are going to be fine. But, thanks for asking." Irene softly said, "Oh, Roger, no matter what, I'll always be here for you." With that, they said goodnight to each other.

Roger was alone but free. And it felt good. He headed upstairs to put what few clothes and toiletries he had away. He put fresh linens on the bed. For the first time in nearly three years, it was truly quiet. Roger liked it but it would take some time for him to adjust.

Chapter 4

"Dead End Streets"

Roger felt a sense of peace as he drank his first cup of coffee on the partially enclosed porch of 2255 N. 33rd Street. He was well rested after sleeping on a real bed for the first time in years. He lingered in the shower for a while. The hot water was cleansing and refreshing. It was as though three plus years of prison stench flowed down the drain. He was actually alone in the shower. No one was watching his every move. There are lots of little ways to celebrate freedom. In the background, Grover Washington's, "Mr. Magic," the title song from Washington's soulful album of the same name played softly. On this first full day of freedom, it was time for Roger to take stock of his life. Because of the conviction, practicing law was not in the cards. Armed with the divorce settlement and having no mortgage, Roger could live comfortably for years and do nothing. He didn't need a job. But living in Sadie's house reminded him that he had an obligation to do something worthwhile with his time.

While incarcerated, Roger had tried to help fellow inmates with their appeals. Everyone claims that they're not guilty but Roger learned that a number of men who had been convicted were actually innocent. Their only crime had been being born Black or Latino and having lousy representation. Roger had vowed "if ever given the chance, I'd help some of these folks." However, since he was no longer a lawyer, Roger's access to the criminal justice system was limited. In the days just preceding his release, Roger pondered if he could secure a job with the Philadelphia Defender's Association as a paralegal/investigator. Thom Dean was running the office. Roger wondered if he could impose upon his buddy for a job. Surely Roger was more qualified than most people hired as paralegals/investigators. He'd call to see if he could get an appointment. Roger was willing to work as a volunteer. But that would be something to pursue tomorrow. Today, Roger simply wanted to enjoy his taste of freedom and try to gauge the vibe of his new-old neighborhood. He also used the time to continue to put things away and get his new home in order. Before getting to these things, Roger went through the exercise routine that he'd started in prison.

After shaving and getting dressed, Roger walked four blocks to 33rd and Lehigh Avenue to the cemetery that was Big Roger's final resting place. Prior to shooting and killing Larry, Roger had purchased a granite headstone from the Veteran's Administration for his father. Roger stopped at the front office of the cemetery to inquire as to whether the headstone had been delivered. He also needed the location of his Dad's plot.

Big Roger and his son had always had a special bond. Many people joked that they looked like twins. A favorite family story was that as an infant Roger would not go to sleep at night until his father came home from work. According to folklore, Roger, Jr., would be placed on his dad's chest. Within minutes, the infant would sleep until the morning.

The cemetery office directed Roger to a particular quadrant. As Roger looked around, the surrounding area looked vaguely familiar. There was a high school football field and baseball diamond just across the street from the cemetery. Despite these landmarks, Roger could not find Big Roger's gravesite. Feeling frustrated, Roger closed his eyes and began to talk with his father. "Dad, you've got to find me, because I can't find you." Roger opened his eyes, took about five steps to his left and looked down. There it was, the headstone that read, "Roger Work, Sr." Roger touched the headstone and said, "Thanks, Dad." Roger laughed and started to clear away some of the clutter that had begun to accumulate around the gravesite. As he was doing so, Roger said, "Dad, I know that you're disappointed in how I handled the Larry thing. But at the time, it was the best that I could do. I was worried about Brandi. You'd be so proud of her. She's grown up to become a fine young woman. I'll never do anything that dumb again." To Roger's surprise, thirty minutes had passed since he had found the gravesite. It was time to move on. He told his father, "Goodbye Pop, I'll see you later." Roger left the cemetery and headed home.

Once back at home, Roger listened and watched the activities in the streets. As Miss Bessie had said, drug dealers seemed to be everywhere. One dealer worked the corner of 33rd and Susquehanna Streets. He appeared to be selling weed and crack. The young fellow he later learned was named Blue. He worked from ten in the morning until late at night. Blue wore low riding baggy jeans and a coat that was too large. Roger suspected that Blue was a mule dealing drugs for somebody. The young man was called "Blue" because his skin was so dark, so black that it almost looked blue. He appeared to be sixteen years old. Blue was a hustler, but hustling on these mean streets always ended up at the same dead end. Roger became a bit melancholy watching him. If this young man had turned his energy towards something positive, he could, one day, run a Fortune 500 company. "What a waste!" Sadly, Blue did much of his business under a beautiful mural of Malcolm X. "What would Malcolm have said to the young brother?" Roger was sure that Malcolm would not have judged him. Instead, he would have made an effort to steer the young man into a better situation.

Roger decided to walk around the park. He returned around 3 pm. At the corner of 33rd and Dauphin Streets was another young dealer named Malik. Malik was different in many ways. Roger learned from neighbors that Malik only worked evenings, four to ten. His business was also brisk, but it didn't seem to be his calling. Also, Malik's pants didn't hang down past his ass. In fact, the kid reminded Roger of the young men who had attended Catholic school back in the old days.

Roger was curious so he approached Malik. "Sup? Whatcha need? I got that chronic." Well aware that chronic was the street term for weed, Roger said, "No. I've been watching you. You don't seem to belong out here." "What? You, 5-0?" "No, I just got out of the joint myself." "Word?" "Yea." Roger told Malik that before going to prison that he'd been a lawyer. Malik looked at Roger like he'd just flown in from outer space. "Well, what do you want from me?" "I just wanted to talk." "Why are you doing this?" "I gotta take care of my Moms." "Do you mean that you're providing food and housing for your family?" "Yea, Jack, what's it to you?" "Where are you going to school kid?" Malik said, "I am a junior at Roman." "Really? I went there too! Well I was just curious. My name is Roger Work and I live up the street." "You, the one that took out Larry up at the B&E a few years back?" "Yea, I am." Changing the subject, Roger asked, "Is Father Finley still teaching at Roman?" Malik smiled and said, "He's still there." "Damn, he must be a hundred by now." Roger said, "Well, okay, see you around." "If I can help, just give a shout."

Malik nodded and returned to his business. While walking back to his house, Roger was sure there was something special about Malik. He'd have to keep an eye on him. Maybe he could help him avoid the falling prey to the streets.

Malik was suspicious of Roger. He had encountered "do-gooders" on other occasions. "Do-gooders" were people who intended to help improve the quality of life of a person or the community but when push came to shove, all they really wanted was publicity – bragging rights. "One Roman Grad to Another," who did this guy think he was fooling. Sure he killed somebody and did time at Waynesburg, but that didn't make Roger one of the brothers. Malik would have to be careful with this guy.

When Roger got back to his house, Eric was there.

"Hey, Roger, can I buy you dinner?"

Roger was appreciative of his gesture and accepted Eric's invitation. Eric introduced Roger to a new area of North Philly. He called it Liberty Square. It was lined with fancy bars and restaurants. They dined at Sovalo. Eric, like Bessie, said, "The neighborhood around the park is going through some changes. As an owner of several chunks of property in the area, I'm confident that soon the drug dealers will move on but in the interim, Roger, you need to be careful.

Don't assume that you can trust any of these young boys who are dealin' on the corners."

Roger thanked Eric for the meal and his advice. They laughed together and reminisced. It was strange how roles had reversed. Eric was eight years Roger's junior. When Eric was a youngster, Roger used to look out for him. He made sure that Eric was not running with the wrong crowd. Eric's brother J.T. was Roger's best friend, and although neither of them were angels, they managed to stay out of any serious trouble. They also did the best that they could to see that Eric did the same. J.T. now worked for his little brother. As Eric talked, Roger thought, "My, how the tables have turned. Eric was a now prosperous business man."

After eating and having a few drinks, Eric brought Roger home. Roger expressed his gratitude and bid Eric good night.

Once in bed, Roger was still wired from the evening's festivities. On balance, it had been a nice day. Roger began to make a list of "to do" things in his head: meet with Thom at the Defender's Association Office, see my probation officer, get a driver's license and buy a used car. Compared to where he had been two days ago, these were nice chores to have. After composing his imaginary list, Roger went upstairs to bed and fell soundly to sleep.

The following morning, Roger took the "A" bus to Center City. He had arranged a meeting with Thom Dean. Upon arriving at 1441 Sansom Street, Roger went directly to see Thom.

Roger was greeted by a receptionist who appeared to be Latina. She answered the phone initially in English but would switch to Spanish effortlessly when needed. She told Roger to "have a seat; Mr. Dean will see you shortly."

The receptionist was an attractive woman, who carried herself very well. Had he been younger, Roger would have described Angela as being as a stone-cold fox-- racked and stacked. She reminded him of J.Lo the singer and actress.

After only a few minutes, Thom emerged from his office and gave Roger a big warm bear hug of a greeting. Thom was still rotund but otherwise he appeared in good health. "Come on in, man. How are you?"

"I'm doing fine for a guy who just a few days ago the state wanted to kill." Thom responded, "Yea, I bet you are. So, what can I do for you?"

"Thom, I learned a lot while locked up at Waynesburg. I'd like to become a paralegal/investigator in your office. Initially, I could volunteer. If you like my work then, maybe, you could put me on salary."

Thom looked at Roger and said, "Is this for real? Man, you were a big-time lawyer once. Would you really throw yourself into this kind of work?"

"I wouldn't ask if I wasn't for real. I want to help and, right now, I don't need money, so yes, I'm as serious as a heart attack. While at Waynesburg, I met a lot of thugs who belonged there but I also talked with plenty of guys who were innocent. They got screwed at trial because of lousy lawyering or because nobody gave a damn. So, I want to help. Clearly, I can't get a license to practice law until my probation ends and, even if I could, I'm not ready at the moment for that kind of responsibility. But, I still want to do something."

"Okay, Roger, I can arrange this. When do you want to start?"

"How about this coming Monday? I still have a few things to do. Everything has happened so fast."

Thom stood and shook Roger's hand. "Okay my friend, I'll see you Monday. When you start, see Angela, and she'll have everything in place. You probably won't see me for a few weeks because I'm starting a murder trial."

"Great, Thom and thanks. You won't regret this. All I want is a chance to save a few brothers from becoming victims of these dead-end streets and the system."

Roger's next stop was to see his probation officer, Sally Hamel. Ms. Hamel did not appear to be thrilled to see Roger. But, she did her job competently. She fired a barrage of questions at him.

"Where are you living?" "Have you found a job?" "How are you adjusting to being outside after three years?"

When Roger told her about his plans for employment, she rolled her eyes. "Really?" "Well, I've got to check this out. Normally, when a person is released, they want to get as far away from the system as possible."

Roger said, "I know. But because of my situation, people may be more comfortable talking with me than some straight-laced guy."

Reluctantly, Ms. Hamel agreed. She then instructed Roger, "If this is on the level, you still have to meet with me once a month and stay away from controlled substances." Roger nodded. "I understand the rules."

Ms. Hamel then asked Roger to urinate into a cup. Never a recreational drug user, staying away from them was no problem. After three years of being locked up, he was used to taking orders. Roger knew that Sally Hamel owned him for the next ten years, so they might as well begin their relationship on a positive note.

When Roger had wrapped up his business with Ms. Hamel, he caught the "A" bus and headed home. When he got off the bus at 4 p.m., Blue and Malik were at their respective stations. All he could think about when he saw the two young men was a book that he'd read years ago entitled, "Man Child in the Promised Land," by Claude Brown. Which one of these young boys would survive like Claude and have a meaningful life? Who would be Pimp and fall victim to the streets? Suddenly, Roger was singing to himself the Intruders' song, "Cowboys To Girls." The transition from adolescence to manhood had never been without perils, now was no different.

Given what Roger had learned from Miss Bessie and Eric, the streets of North Philly were as dangerous as ever. He'd have to watch his back.

Chapter 5

"Me and Mrs. Jones"

Friday morning, Roger took the bus to a city owned parking lot. This was where cars seized by the police during drug raids were stored and then auctioned. Roger was certain that he could get a quality ride for short money. These were cash-only transactions, which tended to limit the number of participants. By 11 a.m., Roger was the proud owner of a 2002 Lexus SUV wagon. It was champagne in color with low mileage. Under the terms of the sale, he had until the end of the business day to get insurance and registration before taking possession of the car. Roger hustled and secured all the necessary items, including a Pennsylvania driver's license. It used to be said that the "eagle flies on Friday, and on Saturday, I go out to play." Roger was soaring and ready to let the good times roll before reporting to his no-paying job on Monday morning. Even a Pro Bono job sure beat the hell out of getting the needle at Waynesburg. Roger was counting his blessings.

On Monday, Angela was seated at her desk when Roger arrived. She reviewed the office's policies and procedures with him. Then she escorted him to his office.

While walking along, Angela stated, "Mr. Work, I'm thrilled that someone with your background is joining our team."

"Thanks!" Roger was appreciative of Angela's orientation and the compliment. The tour was complete, and she was quite pleasant. Roger inquired, "How long have you been with the office?"

"Nearly ten years."

Roger was surprised. Angela looked so young to him.

She asked Roger, "Do you miss being a lawyer?"

"No!"

"Someday I am going to be a lawyer and work in this office."

"That's great, good luck!"

Before leaving Roger's office, Angela gave him several files so that he could begin his work. Roger thanked her. She smiled and said, "You're going to be just fine. If you need anything, my extension is 136." With that, she departed leaving Roger to begin reviewing files.

Roger's first week with the Defender's Association was uneventful. He read documents and interviewed potential witnesses. All of the cases were small-time felonies or misdemeanors, but he felt he had helped and he enjoyed the work. Slowly, Roger began to fall into a routine. In fact, that first week with the Defender's Association reminded him of his first year as a new associate at Coleman, Healy and Tisler in Baltimore. The firm had a policy of requiring its new lawyers to work Pro Bono for the State's Attorney's Office of Baltimore City as a prosecutor.

During this period as a State's Attorney, Roger tried a variety of cases: assault and battery, larcenies, minor drug offenses and burglaries. He learned to write and argue motions to dismiss and suppress. He also became proficient at conducting an effective direct and cross examination of a witness. All of these skills proved extremely useful once Roger returned to the firm. The cases were not the most glamorous, but they were a welcomed chance to hone his skills as an advocate. Back then, Roger took full advantage of the experience. He was doing the same now as a paralegal/investigator with the Defender's Association.

At lunchtime on Thursday of his first week, Angela stopped by Roger's office. "Can I pick you up something for lunch?"

Roger said, "That's kind of you to ask but I'm good."

"Okay."

Roger told Angela again how grateful he was to her.

Angela surprised him by saying, "Mr. Work, I know about your troubles and release from Waynesburg. I know that you killed a man. But, I admire you for not turning your back on your family and not paying someone to do your dirty work. To me, you are a special guy. I will do everything I can to help you here. Just ask. We had a similar situation in my family and no one stood up for my sister. She was beaten badly. Her boyfriend, a gang-banger, broke her jaw and arm and even threatened to burn down the building where she lived. Fortunately he didn't torch the place, but I would have given anything to have had someone like you around."

"Thanks Angela. Coming from you, that means a lot to me. Usually, when I think about my past, I'm not proud of what you are saying."

Angela said, "See you later" and went off to lunch. Roger returned to his files.

Living in Philly, after being away so long, was akin to Roger moving into a new city. He used the weekends to explore the city from the perspective of a tourist.

On the last Friday in February, Thom invited Roger to join him for lunch. Thom had been immersed in a high profile case since Roger had joined the Defender's Association. They had not seen much of each other. Thom's case had been a hit with the tabloids. His client, Katrina Hughes, a self-proclaimed dominatrix, had been charged with killing her customer, Paul Bush, and improperly disposing of the remains. Through credit card slips and dental records the Medical Examiner's Office established Paul's identity and his relationship with Katrina. Fortunately, Thom was able to persuade the jury that Paul died during voluntary consensual sex. Katrina was acquitted of murder but found guilty of improperly disposing of a dead body. She received a $1,000.00 fine for that offense.

Thom was in a celebratory mood. Rarely do public defenders get outright acquittals for their clients, particularly in murder cases. Thom said, "Lunch is on me." An offer that Roger couldn't refuse. Thom drove to Geno's at Passyunk Avenue near Ninth Street. It was an unseasonably warm late February day. Thom ordered a large cheese steak sandwich with the works. Roger shook his head and ordered a medium steak with onions. They grabbed a seat near the stand and began to devour their sandwiches. Thom, in between bites said, "This is the best steak sandwich in the world!" Thom had grown up in South Philly and was thus, partial to Geno's. Roger preferred Pat's steak sandwiches. Pat's had been a staple in his North Philly neighborhood. Pat's also carried a wide array of hot cherry peppers. Just thinking of those peppers made Roger's eyes water. In responding to Thom's declaration, Roger asked, "How many times a week do you eat here?" Thom, with pride said, "As often as I can, it doesn't get any better than this." "Man, you're crazy. This stuff will kill you; it is heart attack city – you'll be sharing space with Mr. Bush if you keep this up." Thom said, "Yeah, yeah. But you've got to die from something and it might as well be a great cheese steak sandwich." Both men laughed. "Seriously man, congratulations on your win. A not-guilty in a murder case. That is amazing." "Thanks Roger. I'm glad that you could celebrate with me. Listen, I'm going to get the authority to put you on salary. The whole process will probably take a few weeks. But I think that we can get it done. Would you like to join us full-time?" "Are you kiddin? I love the work." After wiping the grease from their faces, they climbed into the car and headed back to the office.

At the start of Roger's third month, things changed. As promised, Thom called Roger into his office. "Roger, I've been authorized to offer you a position. The staff is happy with your attitude and work, they support this move whole-heartedly." Roger thanked Thom. Thom then got down to business. "Roger, I have a murder case and I can use your help. Are you ready?" "Thom, you're the boss and I am ready as I'm ever going be." "Roger, by the way, you go on salary starting next week. We pay $40,000.00 a year." Roger said: "Great! Tell me about the case."

Thom began, "Our client is Harrison Jones. He has been charged with killing his wife, Grace Mott-Jones. As you may recall, the Motts are a wealthy Society Hill, blue-blood family. Harrison was born poor and reared in South Philly. Somehow they hooked up, and Harrison was living the life. Normally, our office couldn't -- and wouldn't -- get within two blocks of a guy with this kind of wealth.

Harrison should be worth millions, except for the fact that he's charged with Grace's death. The pre-nup specifically precludes him from touching any marital assets. Our guy is poorer than a church mouse. We think that Grace was about to dump him. But, who knows? Basically, the prenuptial would have left him with bus fare after a divorce. Harrison motive and opportunity – he was home asleep when the body was found. I know that this looks bad, but something doesn't fit. It's not clear that a court would have honored the terms of the prenuptial, so Harrison had a better than fair chance of getting more than chump change after a divorce. More importantly, the police have yet to find any proof of Grace's new "boy toy." However, she was known for slumming. I suspect that there was a new beau, and he would have had a motive if Grace was getting bored with him too. That's millions of dollars worth of motive if Grace's money and her history held to form."

Chapter 6

"Together"

After talking with Thom, Roger took the remainder of the day off. He needed some time to wrap his mind around this new challenge. Prior to leaving Center City, Roger stopped by his alma mater, Roman Catholic High School. By 4 p.m. most of the students are long gone but a few administrators are still around. Roger walked into the Administrative Office to see if he could perhaps catch up with Father Finley. Malik was still on his mind. A male receptionist told Roger that Principal/Headmaster Rev. Finley was still around. Roger could hardly believe it, Father Finily was the "Big Kahuna."

Although it had been more than thirty years, Father Finley recognized Roger instantly. "Roger Work, what a pleasant surprise. It is so good to see you." "It is good to see you too sir, I'm sorry that I embarrassed you and the school." Finley gave him a warm hug and said, "Nonsense, you're always welcomed here." "Thank you Father, I'm in the process of making amends." "I have no doubt, Roger. You were always a responsible young man. I'd expect nothing less. So, why am I honored by your visit today?" "Father, there is a young man living in my neighborhood who I am worried about and I want to help. His first name is Malik. I'm sorry that I don't have a last name but he lives around 33rd Street in North Philly between Susquehanna and Dauphin." The priest smiled, "Roger, I know that young man well. He reminds me of you. He is bright, inquisitive and a hard worker. Anything that you can do to help him would be a blessing." "Well Father, that's my plan or at least, I intend to try. Just to change topics for a moment, how long have you been the Headmaster?" "Roger, you must do a better job at staying in touch. I've held this job for twenty years. I'm sure the reason that I stay is because of little reunions like this. Listen, I hate to rush you but I've got a few things to do before locking things down, but please come by again. More importantly, help Malik." "You can count on that sir." The two men embraced and

Roger was off. As he walked away, Roger realized that he hadn't felt this good in years.

A few days later Malik was on his corner when Roger got off the "A" bus. Although Roger owned a car, parking in town was expensive so to save money and to be energy friendly he used public transportation to go back and forth to work. "Malik, my man, can we talk later?" Hesitantly, "I'll be by in an hour." "Great!" "Hey Mr. Work, Father Finely told me that you came by the school. What's up?" "Malik, we can talk about that later too." "All right, I'll be by soon."

At 10 p.m. Malik knocked on the door. "Okay, so what's up?" "I've got a proposition for you Malik. But, first tell me if I'm right. With your drug dealing, what are you making, $300 a week?" "Yea man, how'd you figure that?" "Well, Blue works full time but, given your hours and commitment to school, your time is limited. But for a 16- year old, $1200.00 a month is not bad." Malik's facial expression indicated that he was uncomfortable with the direction of the conversation. "So, what's your point?"

"Here's the proposal. I'm working for the Defender's Association office as a paralegal/investigator. I could use some help. I'd like to hire you to work with me for $1500.00 a month. The upside is huge. You can continue to help your family and you don't have to worry about getting ripped off, killed or sent to jail. I'm working on a big murder case; I could use your help. So, are you interested?" Malik, with a sheepish grin said, "Mr. Work, are you serious?" "Yes, I am. One Roman graduate to another soon to be grad." "Mr. Work, I like the idea but it's not that easy. I'd have to get permission from my boss and I can't tell you who he is." "Malik, I don't care about your boss. Promise me that you'll consider my offer. An innocent man's life is at stake here." They left things at that. Despite Malik's initial suspicions he was open to the idea of working with Roger. It had been a while since a responsible black male had taken an interest in him. Malik recognized that a relationship with Roger could be just what he needed.

Two days later when Roger got off the bus, Malik was there with a wry smile. "Is that offer still on the table?" "It is. Are you interested?" "Yes sir!" "Well, let's go to my place and talk about the case. Tomorrow we'll meet at the Defender's office after school. I'll tell the folks there that you're interning for me. You'll be paid $1500.00 a month by me and you'll be paid on Fridays starting next week." Clearly excited, Malik said, "Great, let's get started." Roger nodded, "Malik, one more thing, you've got to keep up with your studies in school." "Deal?" "Deal!" "Okay, then let's talk about Harrison Jones." Malik could hardly wait to begin working with Roger. They could be a Philly version of Batman and Robin.

Chapter 7
"Backstabbers"

Roger arrived at the office early the next morning. Carefully, he reviewed the Jones' file to determine where to begin his investigation. About two hours later, Roger and Thom talked. Roger agreed with Thom's instincts. Something didn't fit. "Thom, with your permission, before I start interviewing the people on your list, I'd like to speak with Mr. Jones." "Roger, no problem, all you need to do is present your office identification to the City Correction's Officer and they'll let you see Harrison. Because I'm his attorney, anything said between you and Harrison is protected by the Attorney/Client Privilege. Nevertheless, be careful. To the extent possible, make sure that no one is listening to your conversation. What is it that you hope to learn?" "First, I want to eyeball this guy myself – size him up – hear his story. Most importantly, he's probably going to be our best source in terms of leads. I'm sure that he knew Grace's friends. Those are the people that we need to speak with as to who she may have been seeing on a regular basis. You know that girlfriend to girlfriend thing." "Sounds good to me Roger, just remember, we're scheduled for trial in forty five days."

"Thom there's one more thing. I've hired a student intern at my expense. I want to help this kid. Also, there are likely to be a few places that he can gain access to that I can't. At fifty, it is safe to say that I'm no longer down'. Malik, in addition to being smart, can sort of be an interpreter for me." "Roger, I'm cool with that, but he's your responsibility." "Thanks Thom!"

Malik arrived at the office at 3:30. Angela greeted him and treated him like he'd been part of the team for years.

Roger's office was small. He had a window, file cabinet, a desk and two chairs. Roger told Malik to have a seat. Then they reviewed Harrison's file together. Roger pointed out some of the shorthand used by lawyers and cops when they completed reports. Malik was clearly into it. Roger then made out a list of things that he wanted Malik to work on while he was at the Detention Center visiting with Mr. Jones. Malik was instructed not to work any later than 6:30. Roger asked Malik, "Have you completed your homework?" Malik said, "Yes, my last period is study hall. That's how I balance working and school for the most part." Roger said, "Fine, but remember our deal, school comes first."

Roger then left for the Detention Center to see Harrison Jones. When he arrived there, Officer Tucker was at the front desk. He remembered Roger and wanted to know if he'd forgotten something or "do you just wanted to be locked up again for old times sake?" Roger smiled and showed Officer Tucker his credentials. Tucker whistled; he was impressed. "Okay, so who would you like to see?" "Harrison Jones, sir, please!" "I won't tolerate any funny stuff from you. You're still on probation and normally this kind of thing wouldn't be allowed, but you've got the paperwork so you've got my respect." "Thanks, Officer Tucker. I understand that this all is somewhat unusual." Tucker got on the phone "Officer Desirey, would you please escort Roger to the Attorney/Client room." When Harrison Jones walked in, Roger was surprised. Jones looked very little like his picture. He'd lost weight, his eyes were sunken and he had defeat written all over his face. Harrison was described as six feet tall, brown hair and brown eyes. To Roger he appeared much smaller. When Jones saw Roger he said, "Who are you?" "I'm Roger Work. I work with Thom Dean, your attorney." The men sat down. Roger asked, "How are you doing here? I've never met you but you look tired, emaciated." "Hey man, the noise, smell, the food. I don't know if I'll make it to trial." "Have you seen a doctor?" "Nah." "Would you like to? Maybe he or she can help." "Nah!" "Harrison, listen up. Three years ago, I was sitting exactly where you are. You've got to be a strong man. If guys see that you're weak, things could get a lot worse in here. You know what I am trying to say?" "Yeah! "Why were you here Roger? I mean, what was the charge?"" "Murder!" Harrison's eyes were wide as saucers. He sat up erect. "Really?" "Yes sir, I know what you're going through.

Listen, I think that you've got a chance to beat this. I don't believe that you killed Grace." "I didn't. We'd had a rough patch, but Grace was going to dump this guy Craig. We were going to make a fresh start." Harrison starting to tear up. "I loved her and she loved me and now she's gone." Roger paused, "Can you give me the names of some of Grace's closest girlfriends? Also, do you know Craig's last name and where he lives?" The conversation went on like this for awhile. As they wrapped up, Roger said, "Thanks, okay, I've got some work to do. Harrison remember, you've got to look strong and maintain yourself. We don't want the jury to see someone who looks like a loser. Okay? I'll be back in a few days."

Roger headed home after picking up a few things to prepare for supper and tomorrow's lunch. After he'd finished his meal, there was a knock on the door. It was Eric. Eric said, "Hey, I hear what you done for Malik, that's great." "We need more black men taking an interest in our young men." Roger heard the words, but something about what Eric was saying set his bull-shit meter on high alert. During his years as a lawyer, Roger developed an instinct about people. He couldn't quite put his finger on it. Eric's praise just didn't sit well with him. Roger wasn't buying Eric's jive. Eric asked Roger, "Would you like to get a drink?" Roger passed on the invitation.

Running a little late the following morning, as Roger was waiting for the bus, he noticed that Blue wasn't at his usual spot. He thought nothing more about it as he boarded the A bus. Later in the day, Malik called him. He was upset. Roger could feel his distress through the phone line. "Mr. Work, Blue's dead. They found his body in a vacant lot. Somebody shot him ten times and left him in that lot like he was trash. That ain't right, Blue never hurt anybody." "Malik, you're upset – where are you?" "I am at my crib." "I assume that you've decided not to go to school today." "Yes sir!" "Okay, stay there and I'll come by in a few hours and we'll see if someone knows what's happened." "Sure Mr. Work. Thanks! Blue didn't deserve this!" "Malik, I know. We'll talk later, but I've got to go now. Take today and tomorrow off." Roger turned his attention back to the Jones case.

After carefully reviewing the Jones' file, Roger concluded that his investigation ought to focus on two distinct areas. First, he needed eliminate profit as a motive for murder by examining the financial holdings of Harrison and Grace. From there, Roger intended to begin interviewing the friends and acquaintances of the couple. Additionally, he'd have to go through the "to do" list supplied by Thom.

On the financial side, Roger worked his way through a mountain of income tax returns, credit reports, credit card purchases, insurance policies, stock options and real estate holdings. It was critical to learn if money could have played a role. This wouldn't be the first time that someone had killed to make a quick buck. Roger also determined that Harrison did not have an addiction problem. There was no evidence of a problem with drugs, gambling or women. The couple's 615 Pine Street brownstone still carried a mortgage. The payments for that were made by a Mott Trust Fund.

Roger looked to see if Harrison had made any purchases of expensive items that could quickly be converted into cash like jewelry, a boat, car or vacation home. Nothing came up in his search. Both Harrison and Grace worked. Their combined annual income was in the range of $200,000.00. There wasn't enough in the couple's personal bank accounts to ensure Harrison a life of leisure upon Grace's death. Although Grace's life insurance policy would have guaranteed Harrison enough money for two life times, there was a clause precluding Harrison from getting even a penny if he was implicated in the death of his wife. Roger also looked for dummy companies, investment scams or other vehicles designed to hide assets. He found none. Harrison had luckily married into a rich mainline family with old money, but none of it had rubbed off on him. After meticulously reviewing every financial angle, Roger knew that Harrison had not killed his wife for money. Next, he turned his attention to the list of witnesses supplied by Thom as well as the friends and acquaintances of the couple identified by Harrison. Somebody had been the ultimate backstabber and he was determined to find that person.

Chapter 8

"Only the Strong Survive"

Later that evening Roger's cell phone vibrated as he waited for the bus. According to caller ID, it was Brandi. "Hi Uncle, can you join us for supper on Sunday? My mother is coming in from San Diego for a conference over the long weekend so I'd like to have everyone over for Sunday dinner. Can you make it?" Roger rolled his eyes, "Sure honey. It will be great to see Maria – I haven't seen my sister in a while. Is she happy living out there on the left coast?" Brandi said, "She sounds like she's enjoying life in the sun and fun. We're planning on an extended visit once the kids are out of school for the summer." "Well baby, that's great; I'll be there on Sunday. Would you like me to bring anything?" Playfully she said, "Since you asked, how about some of your white chocolate bread pudding?" "Consider it done; I'll see you on Sunday. Bye." The bus pulled up just as the conversation ended. Roger went directly to Malik's house to see how he was doing. Roger was also curious about what happened to Blue. Malik was waiting on the stairs. He took Roger to the crime scene. The yellow police tape made it easy to find. A patrol car was parked nearby, even though the Crime Scene Unit and the homicide detectives were long gone.

It is an old but familiar story. The relationship between the police and the black community is not particularly good. Roger ever the optimist still decided to try and speak with the officer in the patrol car.

Roger approached. "Good evening sir, the young man whose body was found here was a friend. Can you tell me what happened?" The officer, in a gruff manner said, "Read about in the paper, I'm not at liberty to tell you or anyone else what went on here." Roger said, "Okay sir, I understand, I'm not trying to interfere but Malik and I cared about him." "Look Mister, he was a drug dealer who got what he deserved. Enough said?" Roger thought to himself, so much for the success of community policing. Malik and Roger stared at the spot where Blue's body had laid and started back towards 33rd Street.

As they were walking along, J.T. appeared. J.T. was also visibly shaken by Blue's death, but he was pleased at seeing his childhood pal, Roger. Momentarily, J.T. stopped him. "Roger, my brother, it's good to see you. I'm sorry that I hadn't been by but Eric really keeps me busy." J.T. said, "Hello Malik. Malik, this thing with Blue is bad. I am glad you're out of that world now." Looking towards Roger, J.T. mouthed a quiet "thank you."

Roger said, "J.T., so, do you know anything?" "Man, I know nothing but this is just sad. Another young black man lost to the streets. Roger, please keep an eye on this guy" pointing to Malik. "What I can tell you is that Eric spoke with Blue's mother and he offered to pay the funeral expenses." "That was nice of Eric." "He's not always a cold blooded business man. I've got to get back to work, you brothers take it easy." Malik and Roger bid J.T. goodnight. When Roger and Malik were back at Malik's house, Roger promised "I'll use my contacts at the office to find out what happened." Unexpectedly, Malik hugged Roger and then went into his house.

Friday the office was quiet. Roger did speak by phone with Brenda Chin, one of Grace's good friends, according to Harrison. They agreed to meet at lunchtime on Monday. Roger also asked Thom to inquire into Blue's death.

At 3:00 p.m., Thom came into Roger's office and asked him if he knew that "in addition to the multiple gun shot wounds, that Blue had Crystal Meth on him." "What, are you sure? I knew this kid; all he ever dealt was grass and crack." "Roger, crystal meth is a Class A substance also known as krank or ice. It is made of pseudoephedrine and iodine crystals. Meth is potent and highly addictive." Thom continued, "According to the Medical Examiner, Blue had traces of meth in his system." "Thom, I'm not questioning you or the M.E.'s findings. But, this is wrong. That kid was not into that crap. I'm not even sure he ever used any of that shit that he sold. Blue was an entrepreneur not a junkie. Anyway, thanks Thom. Listen, if you have no objection, I'm going to take the remainder of the day off. Monday I'm scheduled to meet with folks on your witness list plus some of the people that Harrison identified too." "Great Roger, now get out of here, you've earned the right – have a nice weekend."

Blue's funeral service was Saturday morning. The crowd at the funeral parlor was sparse. Malik, Roger and surprisingly, Miss Bessie were the only non family in attendance.

After the internment, Roger took a ride into Lancaster County, Pennsylvania Dutch country, to clear his mind and to sort out his feelings. Speaking to himself "I guess the old neighborhood has changed over the years. I cannot believe the level of indifference concerning the discovery of Blue's bullet riddled body. Blue was no saint. But he deserved better. What a shame – what a waste?"

Chapter 9

"You're a Big Girl Now"

Roger awakened to a beautiful spring Sunday morning. Roger watched the news with Tim Russert and Bob Schieffer. Afterwards, he did a little housework while listening to the baseball game on the radio before heading to Brandi's. His sister answered the door followed by Brandi's three adorable rug rats. There were tons of hugging, kissing and clowning around. Roger asked, "How is life on the left coast?" She indicated, "The new job is great. It pays well and I like the people and the weather."

Maria had not seen her older brother in nearly four years. They were only two years apart in age but different as night and day. Maria had relocated to San Diego, California just prior to Roger killing Larry. Maria was ambivalent about Larry's death. While she and Larry had not seen each other for years, she still had strong feelings for him. This was one of the reasons that she accepted a position with a software company in Southern California. She wanted some distance between her and Larry. Maria recognized that Larry was not good for her. Unlike most of Roger's family and friends, Maria chose not to attend the trial. Larry was the father of her only child and for better or for worse, she cared about him. But Maria loved her brother and was glad that he was out of prison. Maria was certain that in time she would forgive her brother but she'd never forget. As Sadie was fond of saying, "blood is thicker than water." And, Roger was her brother.

Brandi's family dinner was a good idea. For the time being it reunited her fractured family. Maria, in spite of her reservations, accepted the invitation to dinner for she too wanted to end her estrangement from her brother. Whatever Roger's faults, his intent had been to protect her child. Brandi had invited Lenora a friend from her office to join the family for dinner. Lenora seemed nice but Maria was a little cool towards her. Neither Roger nor Brandi knew why. Perhaps Lenora reminded her of Roger's ex-wife who Maria had adored.

Brandi's cooking was superb. Roger left her house around seven and headed home.

The coming few weeks were going to be very busy as the trial date approached for Harrison Jones. Also, Roger was determined to find out what happened to Blue. As an after thought, Roger remembered Brandi's co-worker, Lenora. Brandi's white colleague, Lenora, had been quiet but sociable. She was a widow. Her husband had died in the first Gulf War. She and Roger seemed to hit it off. They were comfortable with each other. Lenora was quite an attractive looking woman, 5'6" about 130 pounds with curly blond hair. Roger guessed that she was in her mid forties. She had grown up in the Boston and moved to Philly with her husband, John. They too were DINKS. According to Lenora, since John's death, she had dated occasionally, but nothing serious. For some reason, just prior to leaving Brandi's, Roger asked Lenora to lunch. Much to his surprise, she said, "Yes." So, in addition to solving two murder cases, Roger would have a date later in the week. The word "date" sounded so funny that he laughed out loud as he drove home. Roger was so proud of Brandi. She wasn't his little girl anymore.

Chapter 10

"Expressway to Your Heart"

Brenda Chin agreed to meet Roger at the Ritz Carlton Hotel's bar at 17th and Market Streets on Monday afternoon. Ms. Chin was one of those women who sucked the air out of the room when she walked into it. Brenda, who is Asian, was tall, lean and drop dead gorgeous. Roger had no problem spotting her when he arrived. She had ordered a Gray Goose martini and was well into it when Roger approached. "Ms. Chin, I am Roger Work. Thank you for agreeing to speak to me." "Mr. Work, it is my pleasure." "I'd like to talk to you about your friend, Grace Mott-Jones." "Sure, Grace and I became friends while we were both at the University of Pennsylvania. Grace was a beautiful person, outside and inside. She loved to party and she loved men. When Grace agreed to marry Harrison, I was shocked. This is no reflection on Harrison. He's a sweetheart and I don't believe that he killed her. I told this to Detective Mearns. However, Mearns seemed more interested in hitting on me than determining who killed Grace." "Wait a minute. You were interviewed by Philadelphia detectives?" "Yes, that's right." "So you don't think that Harrison did this. Why?" "Harrison worshipped the ground that Grace walked on and she loved him. Two days before Grace died, she and I met at the Rose Tattoo up on Callowhill. Grace said that she'd grown weary of her casual relationships. She told me that Harrison had put up with a lot of crap, but she was glad that he had. Grace claimed that she was ready to start a family with Harrison. Apparently, she and Harrison had made peace with their past and were ready to move on to the next phase of their relationship. I can never remember Grace appearing more radiant than she did that night. We laughed and cried a lot that night."

"Grace also indicated that she was going to see Craig Rascotti the following evening to tell him that they were history." Roger asked, "Did you ever meet Craig?" "Yes, I knew most of Grace's paramours," she smirked. "Craig reminded me of the joke about putting perfume on a pig. You know at the end of the day, it smells better but it's still a pig. I know that this sounds cold, but to me, Craig was a low class, south Philly thug. I don't know what Grace saw in him. The guy liked to pretend that he was connected – he'd carry a tire iron around in his car to use as a weapon. One night, Grace asked Craig to walk me to my townhouse. Craig did but he had the tire iron in his hand the whole time. What's up with that?" "Brenda, did you also tell Detective Mearns this?" "Absolutely! Mearns gave the impression that he knew about Craig but that he wasn't interested in him in terms of Grace's death." "Brenda, is there a particular place where you, Grace and Craig would hangout - go for dinner and drinks?" "Yes! Like I said, Craig wanted you to believe that he was some kind of mobster so Frederick's down on Front Street seemed to be his hangout. If a guy looked cross eyed at Grace, he'd jump bad and the staff at Frederick's would have to calm things down."

"Ms. Chin, may I call you Brenda? You've been very helpful. I'm sorry for your loss. Is there anything else that you want me to know?" "No, Mr. Work, just get Harrison out of this mess. He didn't do it." Okay, I'll try and thank you for your time." Roger got up and left Brenda Chin at the bar.

Once outside, Roger called Roman Catholic High School and asked to speak with Father Finley. When Finley answered the phone, "Father, it's Roger Work, I need a favor." Finley said, "Don't worry, I'll make it happen."

Roger then returned to his office. There he met with Thom and laid out his plan. Thom liked it and gave Roger his blessing. Later that day Malik arrived at the office. Roger was glad to see him. He knew that Blue's death still troubled Malik. Roger intended to keep his promise and find out what happened but, in the short run, Malik and Roger needed to concentrate on the Harrison Jones's case. "Malik, I've got a special assignment for you. Please take a look at this photo." Thom had managed to get a picture of Craig Rascotti. Craig had never been convicted of anything serious but his mug shot was on file with the police department. "Memorize the face. Starting next week, you're going undercover to work as a bus boy at Frederick's down on Front Street. You'll work after school and on Saturdays for a few weeks. Father Finley has arranged things. I want you to keep an eye out for this guy Craig. We need to size him up. Is he a player? Might he be Grace Mott-Jones' killer? Can you handle the job for me? You don't need to interact with this jerk, just keep an eye on him and report back everyday, okay?" "Sure, Mr. Work. You know that I want to help." "Great! Well, let's finish setting things up for next week."

Roger and Lenora met for lunch on Wednesday at 1:00. They had previously agreed to dine at a little spot near Rittenhouse Square. Roger was surprised at how nervous he was, however, as soon as Lenora walked in and smiled at him, all of his anxiety vanished. She looked better today than when he'd met her on Sunday evening. Roger asked, "Would you like a drink – some wine?" "I'll have something light and white. Do they have a Pinot Grigio?" Roger got his server's attention and they both ordered.

Lenora said, "Do you think that Brandi invited me to dinner the other evening in the hopes that we might hit it off?" Roger thought for a moment "Anything is possible. But, if she did, I'm glad. So is there anyone special in your life at this time Lenora?" "No Roger – How about you?" "No! Since getting out of prison, all I've done is work. I guess I'm trying to make up for lost time. I'll say this though; I wouldn't mind having someone special. How about you?" "Me too, I think that it's time." "Lenora, do you like music? I mean real music - smooth jazz, Motown and the Sounds of Philly?" Lenora laughed, "Real music. I assume that you're excluding rap and a lot of the hip hop stuff?" "Yes, I am." "Well Roger, I do like the old songs better." "Great, I've got tickets for a show on Friday. Kenny Gamble has pulled together many of the old groups that used to work on his labels for a benefit concert. I've got two tickets, they're great seats. Are you interested?" "Roger, I would love to go." "Then, consider it a date."

Lenora, reading Roger's mind said, "Did you ever think that the word 'date' would apply to you again?" "Honestly, no."

"Well, let's meet at Broad and Locust at 6:30 p.m. By the way, how was your lunch?" "I don't know, I didn't touch mine and neither did you." An hour and a half had gone by in the blink of an eye "We both need to get back to work. I'll see you on Friday. Thanks again for the invitation."

After lunch, Roger contacted several of the witnesses on Thom's list. The results appeared promising but there was no smoking gun. Virtually all of them corroborated some aspect of Harrison and Brenda's version of events. Roger ended the day by attempting to see Homicide Detective Mearns. When he arrived at the Roundhouse, Mearns made it clear that he had no intention of speaking with representatives of Harrison Jones. Mearns' message to Roger was "Hey buddy, go and pound sand, I'll see you in court." Recognizing that this was a waste of time Roger headed home.

As he stepped off the bus Roger thought about Blue. It was still early so he walked over to the storefront that served as headquarters for "Eric's Real Estate and Management Company" to see J.T. The storefront had been the sight of a number of businesses in the past including a pharmacy and a health food store. J.T. greeted his friend warmly. They talked about old times and some of the crazy things that they had done as kids. Both acknowledged that life had not exactly turned out as planned.

J.T. was a gifted musician. He had been the leader of a terrific R&B Band. Sadly however their talent and potential never completely gelled. Nevertheless, J.T. was excited because the Band would perform at Friday's concert hosted by Kenny Gamble. "The Band has been practicing every night and we sound great."

Roger had not heard them perform in fifteen years. To see and hear the Band perform again would be a treat. The conversation shifted to Blue's death –and had J.T. heard anything? Just as J.T. was about to say something, Eric came through the door. They dropped the topic.

Eric asked "what are you doing here?" Roger responded by congratulating J.T. on his upcoming gig. Eric frowned, "That music stuff is all jive, it's not real. That dream dried up on the vine years ago. The real estate business is what pays our bills." Roger was stunned by the level of hostility. Changing topics, he asked Eric, "Have you heard any news about Blue's death?" Eric said, "The boy was a drug dealer – poisoning our neighborhood. He probably tried to rip off somebody and paid the price. Life is hard on drug dealers. Listen, if that's all that you want to talk about, we've got some work to finish before closing, so excuse us please." "Hey, I understand, that's cool, I'll see you Friday, J.T. and good luck."

Once outside, Roger again thought that something didn't feel right. He was certain that Eric knew something. Roger headed home. Later that evening he called Lenora. "Friday is going to be really special because, one of my oldest friends and his band are performing." "That's great." "Lenora, by any chance are you available for dinner Sunday evening? I'd like to take you to the Astral Plane. I think you'd enjoy it." Lenora began to tease Roger, "Are you trying to sweep me off my feet?" They both burst out laughing. Lenora answered, "Yes, I'd love to go out to dinner." "Okay great, I'll see you on Friday, we can talk more about dinner then."

Thursday morning, Roger started his day by visiting Harrison Jones and bringing him up-to-date on their progress with his case. He told him about Brenda, Craig and the undercover operation at Frederick's. Harrison appeared to be in better spirits. After a few more encouraging words, Roger headed for the office. There he continued to do what he could to track down loose ends. Otherwise, Thursday was uneventful.

On Friday afternoon, Malik came in the office and Roger paid him. Malik's smile was so wide and bright that it could have lit up a December night. "Mr. Work, this is the first honest paycheck that I've ever earned, it feels good." "That's good! I'd take you out to celebrate, but I've got a date tonight. I am going to Kenny Gamble's concert.

"You know, to hear some old school music; it probably doesn't mean much to you, Malik." "Hey, come on – I'm from Philly and I like the old school music, too, Mr. Work." "Sorry, Malik I didn't mean to be rude." "Don't worry, Mr. Work, you have a good time. I'm gonna do something special for my mother tonight." "Okay, Malik, remember you're working at Frederick's starting Monday and we'll talk. I hope you'll learn something that helps Harrison. Have a nice weekend." "You too, Mr. Work."

When Roger saw Lenora, his heart skipped a beat. She walked up and surprised him with a tender, but oh, so sweet kiss. Then hand in hand they started walking towards the Performing Arts Center. Roger was floating on air the entire evening. Between the good music and Lenora's good vibes, he was the happiest man in Philadelphia.

Philly's most famous DJ, Georgie Woods, "The guy with the goods," served as MC for the show. J.T.'s band performed at the midway point of the concert. Age had not diminished their skills. Roger was as proud as a new dad. The Delfonics sang their big song "LA LA Means I Love You." They were followed by the Stylistics, who sang "You Are Everything" and "Betcha By Golly." The Stylistics rocked the house as the group launched into several more of their other hit tunes. People were singing and dancing in the isles. Roger and Lenora joined in the fun. It was some night. Roger would remember the evening for a long time.

Chapter 11

"I'm Stone in Love with You"

On Sunday afternoon, after shaving and a quick shower, Roger dressed and set out to pick up his date. When Lenora answered her door, Roger again was struck by just how beautiful and sexy she was. This woman was really hot. His hormones were racing at warp speed. The usually cool Roger could barely say hello. Lenora seeing the internal struggle grabbed Roger's arm, "Are we going to dinner or are you just gonna stand there and continue to act like a fool?" This brought Roger back to earth and he escorted Lenora to his car.

Astral Plane is a neighborhood restaurant. It has been at 18th and Lombard Streets for more than twenty-five years. The restaurant is a quiet, funky and romantic. The motif is right out of Bogart's "Casablanca." Although Roger and Lenora had been spending quite a bit of time together enjoying each other's company, they hadn't really talked about each other's past.

Over supper, they shared stories about loves won and lost. Lenora said, "It's not easy, but perhaps it's time for us to start new lives." She reached for Roger's hand, "I'm ready to begin that journey with you." Their meal was great. They laughed, joked around and drank until closing time. While driving Lenora home, Roger invited her to his house for a home cooked meal next Saturday. Lenora raised her eyebrows, "and you cook too?" She accepted the invitation and asked if she should bring anything. Roger said, "No, I've got it covered, just bring yourself." Before getting out of the car, they kissed. Roger escorted Lenora to her front door. This time the kiss was far from chaste. Both were a little embarrassed by the intensity of it. Roger said "good night. I'll call you during the week. I'll pick you up, or e-mail you directions, whichever is easiest." Lenora threw her head back and said, "Roger, I'll drive. Just have a Stoli and tonic ready when I walk through the door."

Monday, Thom reminded Roger, "There was only a month until trial. Roger would you like to sit with me at Counsel's table?" Roger was honored and immediately said "Yes." After their meeting, Roger went to City Hall for his 11:30 appointment. During his discussion with Brenda, she had mentioned that he should speak with Laurie Tutor, one of Grace's dearest friends. Laurie, a lawyer, worked in the Mayor's office. She was about 5'1", slim, confident, with an infectious smile. Laurie was eager to help. "I saw Grace the evening of her death. Grace and Craig Rascotti were together at Frederick's. Craig was being his usual boorish self. I never cared for Craig, but put up with him because of Grace." Laurie too, had a tire iron story. "One night we were out and Craig was racing for a parking space down at Penn's Landing. Some guy cut in front of him. Craig was bullshit. He reached under his seat and pulled out a tire iron. Then he jumped out of the car and threatened to kill the other driver. Grace and our friends barely got Rascotti under control. I was afraid that he'd kill the poor stiff. I had never been so frightened in all of my life."

Roger asked if she was interviewed by the police. She said no. "Are you willing to testify?" "Yes." "Do you think that Rascotti was capable of harming Grace?" Laurie said, "Absolutely. The man has no impulse control." Roger thanked her for seeing him. He gave her his business card. "Call me if you recall anything else that might be helpful." Laurie asked one final question. "When does the trial start?" "Within a month." "Good luck." "Thanks."

When Roger returned to the office he met with Thom. "Thom, I suggest that you stipulate to cause of death, blunt force trauma, and that Harrison was home. This case will be won or lost on Mearn's investigation and the credibility of Brenda, Laurie and Grace's other friends. Hopefully, Malik will also come up with something while moonlighting at Frederick's." "Well, it sounds like a pretty good plan, Roger, but it's still early. Did I tell you that the District Attorney himself, Mr. Lynne, intends to try the case?" "No! Why is he doing that?" "That's easy, he's got re-election fever." "This is going to be a

circus. Are you sure that you want me at the table with you?"
"Absolutely, Harrison is going to need everything we've got and that includes you."

Malik called Roger Wednesday evening. "Rascotti has been at the restaurant every night. He's like Tony Soprano up in here. Every time he walks in the staff tenses up. It's like they're waiting for him to go off. Do you want me to continue working?" "Yes. This guy might actually be so out of control that he'll say something stupid that we can use in our case so, hang in there a little longer. Have you seen him with a tire iron?" "No, but everyone on his staff seems to have." "Okay, Malik. Keep me posted. Please be careful. Hey man, I've got an extra ticket to the baseball game this Friday. Would you care to join me?" "For real? Sure! I've never been to a professional baseball game." "Great, let's do it. We'll work out the details tomorrow."

On Friday evening Roger and Malik left the office together. They walked towards the subway station where they could hop a ride to Citizens Bank Stadium, home of the Philadelphia Phillies.

Roger had a surprise for his young friend. Not only was he about to see his first professional baseball game but Angela, Thom's assistant, had gotten them two of the most coveted seats in town, through a contact at the Mayor's office. It was a beautiful warm May evening. Perfect baseball weather. Upon entering the ballpark they grabbed a program with a scoring card, hotdogs, popcorn and something to drink. Then they headed for their seats in row two, directly behind home plate. The Phillies were just wrapping up batting practice. Former Rookie of the Year Ryan Howard was taking his cuts.

While the field was being groomed, Roger taught Malik how to keep score. "Malik, have you ever heard of Satchel Paige?" "No sir." "Mr. Paige was a pitcher. He began his career in the Old Negro League. After integration he played for the Cleveland Indians in 1948. Paige was named Rookie of the Year at age 42. Imagine that! He pitched until he was almost sixty years old. Satchel Paige was famous not just for his great pitching but because he was kind of a baseball philosopher. One of Satchel Paige's most famous sayings is 'Don't look back – something might be gaining on you.' Every time there's a close race for a playoff slot towards the end of the baseball season, some announcer will refer to Satchel's, 'Don't Look Back' line. We could both learn something from him.

The Phillies defeated the Nationals by a score of 5 to 1. Malik's new hero Ryan Howard hit two homeruns. After the game they took the subway and bus back to 33rd Street. Roger walked Malik to his house. Malik said, "Thank you." Roger could tell that another person was now hooked on baseball.

Lenora arrived Saturday at precisely 6:30 p.m. with a bottle of wine in hand. As promised, Roger had her Stoli, tonic and lime ready. Lenora took a sip, "Ummm." She set the glass down on a nearby table. "Is that the Stylistics that I hear in the background?" Roger nodded. "Roger, where's the master bedroom?" She reached for his hand. "Show me, please?" He did. And they made love for the first time.

After their meal, which Lenora noted was "Wonderful," they returned to the bedroom for dessert.

Sunday morning Lenora stood on Roger's porch gazing out into Fairmount Park. She was wearing one of Roger's long-sleeved dress shirts as a combination nightgown and bathrobe. "What a beautiful view, Roger, I could stare at this forever." Roger handed her a cup of coffee and kissed her gently. "Yes, this is a nice way to start the day. I prepared breakfast fit for a queen. My lady, breakfast is served."

Lenora finally got on the road at about 5 p.m. Prior to her departure, she informed Roger that she was scheduled to attend a conference in Minneapolis from Tuesday through Friday. Roger offered to take her to the airport and to pick her up when she returned. Lenora said that would be nice, then you could see my master bedroom. Roger smirked, "I'd like that." They kissed and hugged a final time and she drove home. Exhausted, Roger cleaned up. Lenora's scent still filled the air when he went upstairs and fell to sleep.

On Monday at the office, Thom and Roger began to organize the Harrison file for trial. Most lawyers like to have a trial notebook and Thom and Roger were of like minds. The trial notebook would include: the indictment, motions, police and medical examiner reports along with summaries of witness statements and any photographs from the crime scene. It took the better part of the day to assemble the notebook.

Tuesday morning Roger picked up Lenora and drove her to the airport. During the ride he talked a bit about the Jones' case. He wanted to give her some idea of how time consuming a trial, particularly a capital case, can be. Roger anticipated that once the trial started that he'd be pulling a few all-nighters. Lenora said, "I understand. But when you come up for air, put your biscuits in the oven and your buns in my bed." "Count on it." "Roger, how is Malik doing?" "Lenora, I think that he'll be okay but, things are tough right now. I took him to a ball game Friday evening just to get his mind off of Blue. When I was his age, I had the support of my grandmother and dad. Both were strong caring people. Malik is essentially on his own. I worry, but my gut tells me that he'll be fine."

Roger pulled up to the Northwest Airlines departure terminal. He got out of the car and gave Lenora's identification, luggage and ticket to the skycap. Then they hugged and exchanged a disgustingly passionate kiss. "Lenora I think that I'm falling in love with you." With a hand on her hip, "You think? I'll close the deal when I get back."

Chapter 12

"It's Gonna Take a Miracle"

Malik spent three weeks working at Frederick's before returning to the office. He never did see the tire iron, but he was certain that Craig carried one based upon reports. He did see a couple of skirmishes but nothing that required police attention. To put it mildly, Malik thought Craig was crazy. He asked Roger, "What's the term used for people who seem to have no conscience and are out of control?" "Psychopath." "Yeah, that's it. Craig is a psychopath." Roger thanked Malik for his work and told him that he had been a big help. While Malik was keeping an eye on Rascotti's activities at Frederick's, Roger had run a financial check on him. According to the credit report, Craig Rascotti was the owner of an auto repair shop in South Philly. There was a pattern of conspicuous consumption by him that seemed inconsistent with his reported cash flow. Roger thought that he had stumbled across something. Craig's annual income averaged $85,000.00 a year, yet, he was spending around $200,000.00 and there were no outstanding debts. Roger also knew, traditionally, that auto repair shops were ideal places for money laundering. Roger was pretty sure that this is what Rascotti was doing. What was less clear was whether Craig was laundering his own money or somebody else's. In either case, Roger felt that Rascotti was dirty. This meant that Craig was more potentially dangerous than originally feared. Roger was glad that Malik's stint at Fredericks was over now. Malik was in no immediate danger.

With the trial less than a week away, Roger spent another pleasurable weekend with Lenora fearing that they wouldn't hook up again for awhile.

Monday morning at 9 a.m. in the Criminal Justice Center on Filbert Street, the case of Commonwealth versus Harrison Jones was called to order. The Criminal Justice Center is eight stories high. It opened its doors in the late 1990's. Like most new court houses, the courtrooms are spacious and filled with all the modern necessities. The public areas are color coded in a way that's supposed to promote tranquility. The flooring consists of multi-colored mosaics designed to remind one of the calming affects of the sea.

Thom was happy that Judge Nancy Garner would preside over the trial. The judge had the reputation for being firm but fair. She also would not let District Attorney Lynne turn the Jones' trial into a carnival.

Judge Garner ascension to the Common Pleas Trial Court was not without controversy. Nancy Garner had spent ten years in the city's law office when she was appointed to the bench by Governor Rendell to complete the unexpired term of Judge Parker who had died suddenly. Her critics said that she was a "pencil pusher, not a litigator." This was because Ms. Garner had spent little time over that ten year period in the Solicitors office actually trying cases.

Gradually, the noise subsided as case after case Judge Garner demonstrated her proficiency as a jurist.

The bailiff, Mr. Charles Smith, said, "All rise" and the trial began. When Judge Garner came on the bench she got right down to business. "Are there any outstanding discovery issues?" The defense and prosecution in unison, stated, "No, Your Honor ." To both sides she asked, "How much time will this matter require?" The District Attorney stated, "Three weeks. One week to impanel a jury, a week for the government's case, and probably a few days for the defense, then closing arguments." She asked, "Does the defense agree?" Thom rose, "Your Honor, that sounds about right, but, a number of government witnesses, like Detective Mearns, would not speak with my investigator, Mr. Work. So I'm not entirely sure." The judge responded, "Okay, we'll say roughly three weeks, then. Both of you have assistants at your respective tables, who are these people?" The prosecution stood first, "Your Honor, I am aided by Assistant District Attorneys Jason Blair and Carole Hall." Next, Thom said, "Your Honor, with me are the defendant, Harrison Jones and Mr. Roger Work, who is the paralegal/investigator for my office." The judge says, "Thank you gentlemen. Mr. Smith, please read the indictment so that we can determine if Mr. Jones desires a trial." "Yes, your Honor. Would the defendant please rise." Jones stood. "On Indictment CR-2552-06 charging you with Murder in the First Degree of Grace Mott Jones on January 31, 2006, with special circumstances, how do you plead?" "Not Guilty." To the attorneys, Judge Garner stated, "I'm going to order that the jury and all witnesses be sequestered. Is there any objection to that?" The lawyers responded, "No, Your Honor." "I'm also imposing a gag order on all parties. Is that a problem?" "No, Your Honor." "The only thing that I want to see or hear outside this courtroom from any of you is, 'No comment.' There will be no preening and prancing before the electronic media during this trial if I learn that either side has violated my order there will be severe consequences. We've called for 200 people to serve as potential jurors in this matter. We will be seating twelve jurors and six alternates. Initially, I'll greet all the jurors and do a preliminary screening of them for cause. After that we'll do individual voir dire to determine if the jurors are death eligible. As you know, only those who are so opposed to the death penalty that they would never impose it under any circumstances, will be excused. Once completed, I will take questions from each side as we get deeper into the process. Each of you will have ten peremptory challenges. Are there any questions?" There were none. "Would the court officer bring in the first panel of jurors."

Judge Garner gave them a brief synopsis of the case. She introduced the attorneys and their assistants. Garner also went through the list of potential witnesses. She then asked them, "Does anyone have a problem with serving on this case? Does anyone have a relationship with any of the people that I've just introduced?" In this initial group, three people stepped forward. Two people indicated that they were self-employed and the sole bread winners in their families. Both feared that their households would suffer irreparable harm if they were required to be out of work for three weeks. Judge Garner excused those two. The third person stated that she had worked for the Mott family and could not guarantee that she'd be without bias. Garner excused this person as well. She then asked if anyone felt that the police officers were more or less believable than any other witness? Two people raised their hands. Separately they approached the bench. One fellow said that there were several police officers in his family who are honest and he assumed that all other police officers were the same. Judge Garner asked him, "Could he keep an open mind about the facts presented at trial?" He said, "Yes." Garner told him to return to the jury box. The other person, also a male, had the same issue. "Your Honor, I would always give the benefit of the doubt to the police witness." That juror was excused. Lastly, Judge Garner asked about the death penalty. "By a show of hands, how many of you are opposed to the death penalty." Six people raised their hands. Judge Garner said, "Thank you. How many of you would never vote to impose the death penalty, even if the facts and the law dictated that you do so?" Five of the six raised their hands. All five were excused. After a few more general questions, only three of the initial thirty members of the panel were left. They were instructed to return to the jury waiting room. When the jurors left, Judge Garner said to the attorneys, "Clearly, this is going to take some time. Mr. Court Officer, please bring in the next panel." The process was repeated. This time four out of the thirty remained. Garner went through another panel. When they finished with that panel, they had three more potential jurors. It was now approaching 5 o'clock. Judge Garner said, "The court will be in recess until 9 a.m. tomorrow morning. Gentlemen, I remind you that there is a gag order. If anyone violates that order, they will answer to me." Court was then adjourned.

On Tuesday morning, a new panel of jurors was brought in. They were questioned. The second day of jury selection was more fruitful. By the end of the day there were now enough jurors that the judge could accept questions from the lawyers.

By Wednesday, the jury was set -- five women, seven men plus six alternates. The panel was racially diverse. Judge Garner then told the jurors, "You will be sequestered during the trial and you are not to discuss what they heard in court with anyone, including each other." The judge advised them that opening statements would begin tomorrow morning at 9 a.m. "Please bring at least two weeks of clothing and toiletries with you in the morning."

On Thursday afternoon, June 6th, District Attorney Lynne rose from his seat and walked toward the jury box, when he reached the center point, before turning and facing the jury, he said, "May it please the court. Ladies and gentlemen of the jury, the Commonwealth intends to prove that the defendant, Harrison Jones, killed his wife, Grace Mott Jones, in cold blood, on the morning of January 31, 2006, at their Society Hill brownstone located at 615 Pine Street. You will hear the 911 call of Mr. Jones, reporting the death of his wife. Witnesses will also testify that Mr. Jones had been humiliated by his wife on a number of occasions. You'll learn about their expensive taste. This is a case that combines greed and jealousy. Greed and jealousy were the formula that led to murder. At the close of the case, the Commonwealth will ask that you to return the only verdict supported by the evidence, namely that Harrison Jones killed the victim and is guilty of first degree murder with special circumstance. Thank you."

Thom Dean stood. "May it please the Court. Ladies and gentlemen of the jury, my name is Thom Dean, and it is my privilege to represent Harrison Jones who is presumed to be innocent of the charge of murder in the first degree. The evidence will show that he did not kill his wife. The evidence will show that there was a rush to judgment on the part of the police and prosecution. You will learn that the police considered no other suspects but my client. When all the evidence is presented, we will ask you to return the only verdict supported by the evidence, which is not guilty. Thank you."

With opening statements completed, Judge Garner told the jurors, "We will recess until tomorrow morning. You are not to discuss this matter amongst yourselves, or with anyone else. The officers will escort you out of the courthouse and then to dinner. You should avoid all contact with the media, written or electronic. Do you understand? The judge paused. Seeing no reaction, she said, "Get a good night's rest. The real work begins in the morning. Good night." Mr. Smith shouted, "All rise. This court is adjourned until tomorrow morning at 9:00 a.m." The jurors were escorted out of the courtroom.

When the courtroom was cleared, Judge Garner asked, "Are there any agreements or stipulations that will be introduced into the record?" District Attorney Lynne stood, "No, Your Honor." Thom rose, "Your Honor, the defense has offered to stipulate to the cause and manner of death, and that the defendant was home the night of the decedent's death." Judge Garner said, "On its face, that sounds reasonable. But given that this is a capital case, I can understand why Mr. Lynne might want the benefit of the full moral weight of his evidence. I won't order the prosecution to accept the offer." Lynne said, "Thank you, Your Honor." The judge then turned to Mr. Lynne, "Your brother's opening suggested that there was no police investigation. I hope that this is not the case. Or if it is, you better have a darn good reason. I won't hesitate to direct a verdict for the defendant if I'm convinced that the police work in this case was shabby. Do I make myself clear, Mr. Lynne? Okay, gentlemen, tomorrow we'll have the Commonwealth's case in chief." The judge then walked off the bench. The bailiff stood and stated, "Court will be in recess until tomorrow morning."

Two officers escorted Harrison back to lockup. Roger said to Harrison as he was leaving, "We're gonna be okay, just keep the faith." Thom and Roger gathered their things, Roger whispered to Thom, "It looks like we've got a fair shot at avoiding the jury all together." Thom said, "We'll see how the evidence unfolds. I'm sure that Lynne will be discussing things with Detective Mearns before they return to court tomorrow. If I were a betting man, I'd wager that the detective will have a long and uncomfortable night if half of what we know is true."

While Thom and Roger were in court, Malik had begun surfing the Internet to learn what he could about crystal meth.

According to his research, if one could get hold of the chemicals, it wasn't difficult to make. The stuff was highly addictive and appeared to be a drug found in the suburbs and on college campuses. None of this seemed to have any relationship to Blue. But Roger had said, "The medical examiner had found traces of crystal meth on Blue." It just didn't make sense. Blue and Malik's supplier of drugs had been Eric and Eric had never exposed him to crystal meth. Malik was determined to investigate more. The trial offered him a little free time. Malik decided to spy on Eric to see if he could figure out what had happened.

Chapter 13

"Can I Get a Witness?"

District Attorney Lynne met with Detective Mearns immediately after returning to his office. He was angry. "Detective, who are Brenda Chin, Laurie Tutor and Craig Rascotti?" "I don't know Mister Lynne." "Listen Mearns, all three of those names appear on the defense's list of witnesses. Clearly they know something about the defendant, the victim or the crime itself. Are you telling me that you didn't interview any of them?" "No sir! I did speak with the Chin woman briefly but she didn't have much to say, so I didn't give you a report from her." "Mearns, she wouldn't be on the defense witness list if she didn't know something. Before I call you to the stand, you are to investigate these people. I don't like surprises and neither does this judge. If she thinks that we somehow tanked this investigation, Harrison Jones is going to walk. More importantly, both of us are likely to be looking for new jobs. Have I made myself clear detective?" "Yes sir, you have. I'll get on it right away. I'm confident that Jones is good for this, his wife had enough issues to drive any man crazy." "That's what I just told the jury – but, we'd better be able to prove it. I'll see you in a day or so. I'm planning to have you testify after introducing the 911 tape, and calling responding officers and the medical examiner to the stand. At best, that gives you a day and a half to tidy up these loose ends. Mearns, bring me something."

Roger met with Harrison Jones in the prisoner lockup prior to the morning session. "Harrison, I forgot to ask, what woke you up that night?" "Roger, it's a little embarrassing but, every night, at about 2 a.m., I get up to piss. It was late. Gracie said she'd be home before midnight. She said that we were going to start our lives all over again. She said this time we'd do it right."

"When I did not see Grace, I walked down the stairs. The front hall light was lit which was odd. I looked down and there was blood everywhere and Grace was lying in it. I've never seen a dead person except at a funeral or wake. But I knew she was dead. I called 911 and reported that 'my wife was dead on the floor in a pool of blood, please hurry.' The cops arrived in maybe ten minutes, two blue uniforms. They asked me what happened. I told them I don't know, but someone killed my wife."

"Okay Harrison, I'd better get to court. I'll see you upstairs." Roger then turned and said, "Officer." Someone came and allowed him to exit the holding area.

Roger arrived at the courtroom. He sat beside Thom. Ten minutes later, the bailiff said, "All rise."

Judge Garner entered. She asked the court officers to bring in the jury. When the jurors and alternates were seated, Garner said, "Good morning." Then she turned to District Attorney Lynne and said, "Call your first witness." "Your Honor, last evening my brother and I agreed that the 911 call on January 31 could be played for the jurors with the court's permission. Further, we agreed that the call was received between 2:05 and 2:10 a.m. on the 31st. With the court's permission, I'd like to play that tape now." "Just a second, Mr. Lynne," said the Judge. "Ladies and gentlemen of the jury, you are allowed to take notes during the trial. You may not however, share or compare notes with those taken by fellow jurors. Okay Mr. Lynne, you may proceed."

The tape began.

"Hello, 911, how can I help you?" "Oh my God, help me please. My wife is dead. She is lying in our hallway. There's blood everywhere. (Crying can be heard.) Please help me." "Sir, can you repeat that please?" "Yes, my wife is dead and she's lying in a pool of blood in our hallway at 615 Pine Street." "Thanks sir, the police will be there in just a few. Can you open the door without disturbing the scene?" "I think I can." "Okay, then unlock the door and then wait for the officers to arrive." "Thank you, please hurry!"

The tape stopped.

District Attorney Lynne stated, "Your Honor, the

Commonwealth moves that the tape recording be admitted as Exhibit 1." The bailiff placed a sticky tab on the tape recording and marked it G-1. Judge Garner looked at Thom. "I assume that there are no objections?" Thom stood, "That is correct Your Honor." "Okay, then it is officially government's Exhibit 1."

District Attorney Lynne next said, "The Commonwealth calls patrolman Zack Taylor." Taylor looked like someone who had played football or basketball. On the streets, Taylor and James, partners, were known as Batman and Robin. Taylor, who is white, played college ball at Saint Joseph's College. James, who is black, graduated from Gratz High School in North Philly.

Officer Taylor took the oath. After a couple of preliminary questions he testified, "My partner, Patrolman James and I responded to a 911 call at 2 a.m. on January 31, 2005. That directed us to go to 615 Pine Street. When we arrived we were greeted by the defendant, Harrison Jones. He was very upset. There was a dead body on the floor and lots of blood. I took Mr. Jones to the kitchen in the hopes of calming him down. While there we waited for the medical examiner and our crime scene unit. My partner waited in the living room area. I offered to make some phone calls for Mr. Jones but he indicated that he'd make the calls later."

When Attorney Lynne finished with Taylor, the court asked Thom if he wished to cross examine. Thom said "No, Your Honor"

Officer James testified next. His testimony mirrored Officer Taylor's. Thom also declined to cross examine him.

Mr. Lynne, who is your next witness?" "The State Medical Examiner, Your Honor."

Judge Garner, said to the jury, "It's 11:45 a.m. Let's recess here. Ladies and gentlemen of the jury, we're going to break for lunch now. You are to be back in the jury room before 1 p.m. Remember, do not discuss this matter with anyone, including each other. Would the court officers lead the jury away to their lunch at the Reading Terminal?" The terminal has a number of cafes and restaurants with a wide enough array of comfort food to satisfy anyone's taste's buds. The jury was led away.

Once the jury had cleared the room, Judge Garner turned to Mr. Lynne and said, "All of the evidence that was just presented could have been addressed in a stipulation that you declined to accept. I am warning you, if the Commonwealth doesn't present proof of a connection between the decedent's death and the defendant, I will direct the verdict in favor of Mr. Jones. Am I clear sir?" "Yes, Your Honor. The Medical Examiner and Detective Mearns, who we anticipate calling tomorrow, will take care of these problems. I was just setting the stage." Judge Garner stated, "It looks to me like you are stalling, attempting to buy time, but I won't prejudge your case. Simply consider yourself warned." Garner banged her gravel. "The court will be in recess until 1:15 p.m." And then the judge stalked off the bench.

Roger said to Thom, once they were outside the courthouse, "She's right, Lynne is tap dancing. He doesn't have the goods." Thom looked at Roger, "You may be right but let's not count our chickens before the eggs have hatched." If you're correct, Mr. Jones will be a free man in a day or so."

While in chemistry class, Malik kept thinking about Blue and the Crystal Meth. He approached his teacher. "Father, please don't get the wrong idea but, from a chemistry standpoint, how difficult would it be for a person to manufacture Crystal Meth?" "My son, that's the problem with this terrible drug, it is relatively easy to manufacture if you have the chemicals and a place to mix them. It is cheap to make with a very high profit margin. Crystal Meth has a much higher street value than pot, crack or even heroin. A dealer can charge a lot more. The high from this stuff can last upwards to eight hours. It is also highly addictive so once a person gets started, they become a regular customer for life. Meth is easy to make if the right chemicals are available."

After the luncheon recess, District Attorney Lynne called Chief Medical Examiner, Dr. Marie Myers to the stand. D.A. Lynne began.

Q.   Please identify yourself.

A.   My name is Marie Myers. I am a pathologist and the Chief of the Medical Examiner's Office for the Commonwealth. My office is here in Philadelphia.

Q.   Where were you educated?

A.   My undergraduate degree is from the University of Pennsylvania. I attended Harvard   Medical School. My residency in Pathology was at both the Massachusetts General Hospital in Boston and the University of Pennsylvania Hospital here in Philadelphia. I worked as an Assistant Medical Examiner in New York City and Washington DC for ten years before accepting the position of Chief here in Philadelphia.

Q.   Did you examine the remains of Ms. Grace Mott-Jones?

A.   Yes.

Q.   When?

A.   Initially, on the morning of January 31, 2005, at the scene of the crime. I was on call that night so I responded to the scene to supervise the removing of the body and the collection of evidence. The police department's Crime Scene Investigative Unit was also present.

Q.   Please describe for the jurors what you observed.

A.   Upon entering the house, I observed what appeared to be a white female in her late twenties to mid thirties lying face down in a pool of blood. She was identified by one of the police officers as being Grace Mott-Jones. Closer examination revealed gashes and lacerations about her head and shoulder. Her blood soaked her hand and forearm. Both were bruised, consistent with a defensive wound. Without an autopsy, I was unable to determine the total number of wounds, but there were many. I tested the body temperature and made a preliminary determination that Ms. Mott-Jones had been dead less than four hours. I arrived at the scene between 2:30 – 2:45 a.m. Blood spatter in the hallway appeared to flow from left to right.

Q. Did you make a preliminary finding as to cause and manner of death?

A. Yes – it appeared that death was caused by a blunt trauma. The manner of death I believed was homicide.

Q. What other preliminary observations, if any, did you make?

A. There appeared to be hand prints on both sides of the wall.

Q. Did you take any action regarding the prints?

A. Yes, I suggested to the crime scene techs that they take photos of everything around the   body and walls. I also asked that a finger print expert go over the entire area.

Q. Did you see Mr. Jones?

A. Yes, briefly. He had a small amount of blood on his trousers.

Q. At some point, did you conduct an autopsy?

A. Yes, on February 1st at 11:00 a.m.

Q. Go on please.

A. I began first with a visual inspection of the remains. There were six contusions in the head area. I also examined more closely, what I initially thought were defensive wounds. My external examination also included determining the height and weight of the decedent, I took pictures before starting the internal examination. I made a Y incision, cracked open her chest, examined and measured the vital organs: her heart, liver, lungs, kidney and stomach. All of which appeared to be normal. The contents from the stomach and the temperature of the body confirmed that the victim had not been dead for more than a few hours. There was a great deal of blood inside the body cavity suggesting that the victim bled for some time. She did not die immediately from her wounds. It is likely that the

66

victim was unconscious early into the beating. I carefully examined her skull area and reflected the skin. The injuries were consistent with a slim rounded object. I could tell this from the bevels left on the skin and bone. There were also traces of an unknown metal on the skin of her skull and the skull bone itself. The blows were administered in a downward manner suggesting that the assailant was 3 to 4 inches taller than the victim. I also concluded from the angle of the wounds that Ms. Mott-Jones was struck from behind several times. She attempted to ward off the attacker and that's how she sustained the hand and forearm injury. It is apparent that the first blow did not kill her. It is difficult to tell which of them actually caused death. It is clear, however, that shortly after sustaining the defensive wounds, Ms. Mott-Jones was not conscious. There is an injury to the left side of her temple area. This is probably when she passed out. It is likely that all of this happened quickly and that she was surprised.

Q.   What is your official determination as to the cause and manner of death?

A.   Same as the preliminary death by blunt for a trauma – by person or persons unknown. This is a homicide.

Q.   Did you speak with Detective Mearns?

A.   Yes, I gave that detective a copy of my report. I told him that whoever did this was likely to have had a lot of blood on them given the splatter pattern I observed at the scene. I told him we were still awaiting the toxicology's report. This might reveal something. Lastly, I told him that it appeared to me that the victim had dined at an Italian or Mediterranean type place given the content of her stomach.

Q.   Have you talked with the Detective since then?

A.   No.

Q.   Is that unusual?

A.   Not necessarily.

District Attorney Lynne said, "Thank you doctor. Your Honor, at this time, the Commonwealth moves that the Medical Examiner's report be entered as Exhibit 2 and that it be published to the jury."

Judge Garner asked Thom, "Is there an objection?"

Thom rose and said "No, Your Honor."

"Mr. Lynne, are there any more questions for this witness?"

"No, Your Honor!"

"Does the defense wish to cross examine the witness?"

Thom stood, "Yes, Your Honor. May I approach the witness?"

"Yes you may."

Q.   Good afternoon Dr. Myers.

A.   Good afternoon Mr. Dean.

Q.   Doctor, I have a few questions. Early in your testimony, you said the blood spatter pattern was left to right is that correct?

A.   Yes!

Q.   Doctor, do you have an opinion based upon the facts whether the assailant was left or right handed?

A.   Yes, I do.

Q.   Please tell us your opinion.

D.A. Lynne objected. "Your Honor. The Doctor is an expert on cause and manner of death, not whose left or right handed."

Judge Garner overruled his objection. "She can answer if she has an opinion."

A.   Mr. Dean, in my opinion, the blows were administered by someone who was left handed.

Q.   Doctor, are you aware of the fact that the defendant is right handed?

A.   No.

Q.   Doctor, on the morning of the 31st you saw my client. Is that correct?

A.   Yes.

Q.   Was there blood all over his clothing?

A.   No.

Q.   Based upon your brief visit to the house at 615 Pine Street, did you observe blood anywhere other than the vestibule?

A.   No.

Q.   Did you ever learn the results of the finger printing analysis?

A.   Yes.

Q.   What was discovered?

A.   The prints of the decedent, your client, and other unknown persons were recovered from the scene.

Q.   Doctor, directing your attention to the shape or impression of the wounds, is it possible that those injuries would have been inflicted with a tire iron?

A.   Yes, the wounds are consistent with any object of that shape and size.

Q.   If a tire iron was used as the weapon, is it possible that it would leave the traces of metal you described?

A.   Yes.

Q.   Finally, Doctor, to your knowledge, did the police search my client's home?

A.   Yes.

Q.   Did they find an object consistent with the injuries in your report?

A.   No.

Thom: Your Honor, I have no further questions of Doctor Myers.

Court: Mr. Lynne, do you wish to redirect?

Lynne: No Your Honor.

Court: The witness is excused. Mr. Lynne, your next witness please.

Lynne: Your Honor, the Commonwealth intends to call homicide Detective Mearns – but, I told him he wouldn't be needed until tomorrow morning.

Court: Approach the bench gentlemen.

"Mr. Lynne, you guessed wrong – you had no right to do so. I could find the defendant not guilty right now if that's all you intend to present. However, because there's been a death, I'll give you until tomorrow."

The court turned to the jury – "Ladies and gentlemen, this completes our work for today. The court officers will take you back to your hotel and then out for a very nice meal. In the meantime, I'm going to have a talk with the lawyers. I'll see you in the morning at 9 am. Remember, you are not to discuss the case with anyone. Good night."

The jurors stood and were escorted out by a court officer. When they were gone, Judge Garner said "before we waste another day, I want an offer of proof from both sides as to what your witnesses are expected to say. Mr. Lynne?"

"Your Honor, Detective Mearns would begin with his credentials. Then he would tell the jurors that in his experience where there's been a murder, the surviving spouse is always a suspect. Because of this fact, Mearns immediately turned his attention to Mr. Jones. He learned that this was a bad marriage. Ms. Jones frequently stepped out on her husband. After three years of marriage, he was fed up. There was a confrontation and Jones killed his wife and made it look like somebody else did the deed. Mr. Jones has no alibi and he admits to being home. It strains credibility to believe that he wouldn't have heard something given the kind of beating that was administered to the victim."

The Judge turned to Thom, "Mr. Dean, your offer of proof?"

"Yes Your Honor. We have two witnesses who are old friends of the decedent. The first, Ms. Chin, spoke with Detective

Mearns. She went to college with the victim. She is well aware of Ms. Mott-Jones liaisons. What she will testify to is that Ms. Jones told her a few days before her death that she loved her husband. She intended to save their marriage. The she wanted to have children with the man. She will also say that she knew Ms. Jones' last boyfriend. Chin believes that he's a dangerous guy. He is tall, about 6'2". She saw him pull a tire iron out from the front seat of his car and threaten to kill someone. She will testify that he was extremely jealous, possessive and short tempered. Ms. Chin also knows of the restaurant frequented by this last boyfriend whose name is Craig Rascotti. Lastly, Ms. Chin knows Harrison, my client, and she doesn't believe that he'd harm his wife. Your Honor, Ms. Chin also shared all of this information with Detective Mearns.

"Our next witness is Laurie Tutor. Ms. Tutor is an attorney in the Mayor's office. She too had been a friend of Ms. Mott-Jones for years. She knew about Mr. Rascotti as well. Indeed, the night of the murder, Ms. Mott-Jones was meeting Craig Rascotti at Frederick's on Front Street to break off their affair. Ms. Tutor was with the victim and Rascotti for part of the evening. Tutor will testify that Rascotti is left handed. She also has her own tire iron story that frightened her. Needless to say, she doesn't believe that the defendant killed his wife."

"Thank you, Mr. Dean. Mr. Lynne, On the basis of this offer of proof, I'm prepared to sign a search warrant for Mr. Rascotti's car. If the tire iron is found in the location alleged, it should be tested. If there is human tissue, then the DNA test should be run immediately. Obviously, if there's a preliminary match, I expect you to agree with Mr. Dean on a motion for a required finding of not guilty. Are there any objections?" No one said a word. "I didn't think that there would be. Mr. Lynne, when the paperwork is ready, I'll authorize the search warrant. You have until 5:30 p.m."

Judge Garner then announced, "Court is in recess until 9 a.m. tomorrow. The bailiff said "all rise. Court is now adjourned." Lynne and his colleagues flew out the courtroom.

Thom turned to the court officer and asked for a few minutes to explain to his client what happened. "Harrison, normally, trials are not like Perry Mason but this case is. If they find the tire iron and there's still tissue on it then, you're going home soon. But, don't get too excited. Things could still go sideways on us. Tomorrow should be fun even if Mearns testifies because we know for sure that he conducted a half ass investigation." Harrison seemed pleased but confused. Thom and Roger then left the courthouse.

Malik worked his way into an abandoned home across the street from Eric's newest rehab project at 32nd and Ridge Avenue. He had borrowed some binoculars from the office. Unlike most people, Malik learned how connected, cruel and greedy Eric really was when he had been a drug dealer for Eric along with Blue. Eric seemed to have the police in his pocket. Malik had been observing for about an hour when he saw Craig Rascotti pull off to the curb. He said to himself, "What the hell is he doing here?" Eric showed up moments later. Eric directed Rascotti to park his car in the alleyway between the row houses. It was now dark. Malik waited to see if any lights came on in any of the vacant rehabs. When he saw a basement light come on, he crossed the street and peeked into a window. Eric was handing packages that looked like drugs to Rascotti. The drugs were not packaged in the way that Malik and Blue used to get their stuff. Rascotti then gave Eric money. When the light was extinguished, Malik hurried back to his hiding place. Rascotti pulled out of the alley and drove away towards downtown. Eric walked back to his storefront office. Malik said, "Well, I'll be damned."

Prior to the jury being brought back court resumed. District Attorney Lynne said, "Judge Garner, my office would move along with the defendant for a required finding of not guilty. New evidence has been found that exonerates Harrison Jones." There was a buzz from the media section of the courtroom "Furthermore, Mr. Craig Rascotti is now in custody. We've charged him with the murder of Grace Mott-Jones and trafficking a Class A substance, Crystal Meth. Your Honor, the police found two pounds of Meth in his car. The street value would be over $100,000.00. All of this was found during the execution of the search warrant. We also recovered a tire iron that was stained with blood.

Judge Garner said, "Mr. Jones, you are free to leave. On behalf of the Commonwealth, I apologize for this terrible injustice. This court is adjourned!"

Harrison, Thom and Roger were backslapping and high-fiving. It was all over. Thom, never a man to pass up a chance to eat, offered to take everyone for a late breakfast to celebrate. Roger's cell phone vibrated fifteen minutes later. It was Lenora saying "congratulations honey, we'll talk later and have a private celebration." Roger laughed. Thom asked, "Is that your squeeze? Damn, good news travels fast."

"Well, gentlemen, Thom said, "let's go have breakfast." Harrison said, "Roger you mentioned that young high school fella was instrumental in the outcome. Is there any way that I can thank this young man?" "He's a junior at Roman. Hopefully, he'll go to college. Perhaps you can help with his first year's tuition." "I'd be honored to do something like that, just stay in touch Roger. I'd be pleased to help. I owe this young man my life."

Roger spoke with Malik at 3:30 p.m. and reviewed what happened. He told Malik about Rascotti's murder and drug charges too. Malik was happy for Thom, Roger and Harrison, but he seemed distracted. Roger stated, "Malik, tomorrow night, you'll meet my girlfriend and we'll all have dinner at some fancy restaurant. "Okay?" "Sure Roger!"

Chapter 14

"There's Gonna Be A Showdown"

Lenora and Roger arranged to meet later in the evening. He left his office a little after 5 p.m. The ride home on the A bus line seemed to take forever. Roger found a note stuck to his front door. He recognized Malik's handwriting instantly. In it Malik apologized for letting him down. Malik wrote "I'm pretty sure that Eric killed Blue and I intend to find out why. He also admitted that he and Blue had been drug runners for Eric." Roger had suspected this. Malik said that "I'm going to see Eric at his 32rd and Ridge Avenue redevelopment site." Roger dropped the note and started running. On the way he stopped by Miss Bessie's. "Miss Bessie, if I'm not back in half an hour, please call the police and send them to 32nd and Ridge." Bessie said, "What's wrong Roger?" "I can't really explain now but if I don't hurry, Eric is gonna kill Malik. Please just do as I ask." She nodded and Roger was off and running again. He could hear his heart pumping as he raced the two blocks. Roger could not shake the feeling of dread. If Malik died it would be his fault. It was Roger who had ignored the warnings from Eric. Roger had talked Malik into working with him. Roger was just another "do gooder" doing more harm than good. Quietly he prayed that it wasn't too late.

It was nightfall as Roger ran by the block where the housing was in various stages of repair. He looked for any flicker of light. At the last house on the block, the basement was dimly lit. Roger sprinted past the unit to the alleyway where the back yards for the row houses were located. Roger spotted Eric's car. Drenched with perspiration he hurried back to the front of the building. Roger knelt on the ground and attempted to look through the dust and grime covered basement window where he had seen the light. Two men were in the basement. One was standing over the other. Stealthily Roger entered the house towards the basement. Before descending the stairs, Roger shouted "Eric, are you down there?" "Yeah, my brother, come on down. I'm just finishing up a little business." Cautiously, Roger stepped down the stairwell. First, he saw Eric smiling with a gun in his right hand. Malik was on the floor bleeding, but alive. Eric said, "I have been waiting for you. We're all gonna take a ride." "Eric, I don't understand." "Roger, you're a liar and not a very good one for a lawyer. I told you to stay away from these young boys, but you wouldn't listen. I gave you this one. I figured that would satisfy whatever need you had to fix the world." Eric sneered, "I figured that Malik wouldn't dime me out because he knew that I'd hurt his family. Malik, did you keep our little secret?" The young man nodded his head.

"Roger I have a good thing here and now you're messin with my shit. Sure I had a few kids hustling dope for me, but that wasn't where the big money was. I was using the rehab of these old houses as a cover for my crystal meth labs. That crap I could sell in the suburbs to the white kids and college punks like you. Malik's boy Blue figured out what I was doing and the bastard tried to shake me down. Can you imagine? So I killed him. You know the rehab and de-leading process was the perfect cover for running a floating meth lab. Hey, the government was paying me to remove lead from these houses that I bought and fixed up and I used the system to front my own business. What a country! That damn Blue nearly upset everything. Now I've got you two sticking your noses into my business. Like Blue, you've got to pay. Boys, it is time to take a ride. So here's what's gonna happen. Roger, you're going to help the kid walk up the stairs and head to the alleyway. We can't have too many dead bodies turning up around here. Even thought I have cops on my payroll, it just wouldn't be good for business. Roger, you'll drive. If either of you tries something stupid, I'll blow your brains out, torch the car and walk away." The three men paraded up the stairs and out the back of the house to the alleyway. Eric stood a foot behind them. When they got to the car, Miss Bessie was standing there. Eric said, "Good evening, Miss Bessie, isn't it a little late for you to be out here?" "Eric, is that you boy?" "Yes, Ma'am. Roger, Malik and I are going for a ride." Miss Bessie said, "I don't think so." Eric turned and faced the elderly woman but before he could say anything else, she shot him twice. Eric fell to the ground. Roger and Malik's eyes were as wide as saucers. Miss Bessie said, "You two get out of here, now."

After they fled, Miss Bessie turned to Eric and said, "I promised Sadie that I'd look after her grandchild. My granddaughter, Dawn, died from an overdose that she got from one of your people. When the ambulance arrives, you tell them whatever you want – except the truth. Do you understand? If not, I'll finish the job now." Eric was crying in pain from his wounds. Sirens could be heard in the distance.

"You punk! When Sadie and I first moved to this neighborhood, it was beautiful. But not everyone welcomed us. The Klan attempted to run us out. We scared them off along with our Jewish neighbors, but we learned a lesson. Our husbands took us all to the firing range and taught us each how to use a gun. They also made us promise never to let the kids know. We didn't, but when we girls got together at Sadie's house, we'd just laugh about those sessions. Then we'd toast to our beloved husbands. Well, I am eighty, but there's nothing wrong with my vision or my aim, so don't come back. Turn the housing business over to your brother, J.T., or you'll go to hell tonight. Do you understand, boy?" Eric nodded. "Goodbye Eric."

Epilogue

"The Power Of Love"

Eric survived his gun shot wounds and moved to some unknown location on the West Coast, J.T., continued the work of revitalizing the neighborhood that had been started by Eric. The amount of drugs on the street dropped dramatically.

Roger took Malik to the hospital the night of the shooting but he was released with just a few stitches. After Malik was discharged from the hospital Roger told him that Harrison Jones had offered to pay his first year of college tuition.

The next evening, Brandi came by to visit. Through the grapevine, she learned about the prior evening. Miss Bessie stopped by to see Roger. While she was there, he offered both a beer and a drink. Bessie graciously accepted but, Brandi declined.

Roger thanked Miss Bessie for saving his and Malik's life. Bessie said, "Child don't thank me, thank your grandmother, Sadie. She was proud of you and she loved you. Just think of last night as Sadie's wrapping her arms around you." "Okay. Do you mind if I bend an elbow and join you for a drink?"

Bessie said, "No lady likes to drink alone. Can I assume that you two will never forget about the power of love." Brandi said, "Yes, you're right about that." Roger did join Miss Bessie in a toast to Sadie.

The author thanks Mural Arts for allowing him to use the Malcolm X Mural.

The Mural Arts Program (MAP) is the nation's largest mural program. Since 1984, MAP has created over 2,700 murals and works of public art, which are now part of Philadelphia's civic landscape and a source of inspiration to the thousands of residents and visitors who encounter them, earning Philadelphia international recognition as the "City of Murals." MAP engages over 100 communities each year in the transformation of neighborhoods through the mural-making process. MAP's award-winning, free art education programs annually serve over 2,500 youth at sites throughout the city and at-risk teens through education outreach programs. MAP also serves adult offenders in local prisons and rehabilitation centers, using the restorative power of art to break the cycle of crime and violence in our communities. For more information about the Mural Arts Program please visit www.muralarts.org.

Special thanks to Donna Desirey, Ele Jaynes, Candee Cintron, Jerry Healy and Chanel Ward Richardson. Without all of you, I never could have completed the project. A shout-out to Attorney Laurie Bennett who helped me with editing and the Baltimore portions of this story.

About the Author

Robert Ward is the dean of Southern New England School of Law. He was born and raised in Philadelphia, Pennsylvania. Ward earned his B.S. from Northeastern University and J.D. from Suffolk University School of Law. He and his wife of thirty years live on the South Shore of Boston.

www.ingramcontent.com/pod-product-compliance
Lightning Source LLC
Chambersburg PA
CBHW031953190326
41519CB00007B/780